COME
AWAY
WITH ME

Pray! Magazine's

GUIDE TO PRAYER RETREATS

The Navigators is an international Christian organization. Our mission is to advance the gospel of Jesus and His kingdom into the nations through spiritual generations of laborers living and discipling among the lost. We see a vital movement of the gospel, fueled by prevailing prayer, flowing freely through relational networks and out into the nations where workers for the kingdom are next door to everywhere.

NavPress is the publishing ministry of The Navigators. The mission of NavPress is to reach, disciple, and equip people to know Christ and make Him known by publishing life-related materials that are biblically rooted and culturally relevant. Our vision is to stimulate spiritual transformation through every product we publish.

ISBN-13: 978-1-60006-294-0
ISBN-10: 1-60006-294-6

Cover design by Bridget McNamara

Some of the anecdotal illustrations in this book are true to life and are included with the permission of the persons involved. All other illustrations are composites of real situations, and any resemblance to people living or dead is coincidental.

Printed in the United States of America

1 2 3 4 5 6 7 8 / 12 11 10 09 08

Dedicated to the memory of my husband, David, who died one day before the manuscript for *Come Away with Me* was due. David always did whatever it took to free me up for a prayer retreat, and for that I will always be grateful.

CONTENTS

INTRODUCTION

I n past generations there doesn't seem to have been much written about prayer retreats. I have a theory on that. I think prayer retreats weren't mentioned much because they weren't as necessary; past generations were better at following the Fourth Commandment than we are. For them, every Sunday could have been a prayer retreat of sorts.

Many Christians in my grandparents' day and age were strict Sabbath keepers. But I'm not very good at Sabbath keeping at all. As the full-time editor of *Pray!* magazine and up until recently the primary caregiver for my seriously ill husband, the weekend never seems to be enough time to finish everything I need to do before Monday morning rolls around again. I haven't seen a Sunday-afternoon nap in decades. And time for extra prayer and reflection? Hardly.

My circumstances are probably different from yours. But nearly everyone these days is overscheduled and weary, it seems. I'll bet most Christians who have picked up this book haven't enjoyed a good Sabbath rest in a long time, either.

I can't prove it, but I wonder if we as contemporary Christians were to enjoy God's gift of Sabbath more regularly, perhaps there wouldn't be a need for this book. But since most of us don't, I suspect most of us are desperately need a leisurely spiritual rest and a break from our hectic daily lives.

I'm not saying these things to make anyone feel guilty about the Sabbath. What I am saying is, most of us desperately need spiritual rest and refreshment. And one way to get that is to make time for regular prayer getaways with God. Could regular prayer retreats be one way for us to get the spiritual rest God intended?

I talk to lots of people who admit that a prayer retreat sounds like a good idea in theory, but for many of them it appears difficult in practice. They wonder how they could justify taking the time away from their many responsibilities. And even if they could somehow find the time, they wonder how they could possibly pray for a whole day. They wonder where they would go, and if there really are enough benefits to make the sacrifice worthwhile.

This book addresses those questions and more, and makes prayer retreats accessible to everyone. If you've never been on a prayer retreat, you'll discover here everything you need to get started. But even if you're a pro at prayer getaways, you'll still find lots of fresh ideas to inspire future times alone with God.

Some of the stories and ideas in this book are culled from the best *Pray!* and *Discipleship Journal* magazines had to offer on the topic. The rest of the material comes from my own years of experience at getting alone with God for extended times of prayer. As you read this book, my prayer is that you will not only hear God's invitation to "Come away with Me" for yourself, but that you also will take Him up on it.

Chapter 1

A GRACIOUS INVITATION

D o you ever feel burned out from serving your family, your church, your boss, even the Lord?

Does your relationship with God ever feel less close and personal than you'd hoped it to be?

Do you ever get bored with your prayer life?

If you answered yes to any of these questions, this book is for you.

Many of us—including and perhaps *especially* those of us in ministry—often find ourselves overwhelmed, distracted, exhausted, lacking spiritual power, and near burn out. We give and give and give, barely ever making time to refresh and renew ourselves.

Most of us also—busy or not—long for deeper intimacy with God. We may have disciplined ourselves to a regular habit of Bible reading, prayer, and service, and yet we don't feel as close to God as we'd like to. We know God is our Father and closest friend—we just want to experience Him more regularly and deeply.

Still others of us are bored with our prayer lives. Our prayer lists don't inspire us the way we'd like them to. Our prayer forms are worn and don't engage us like they used to. We feel guilty for our lack of enthusiasm but don't know what to do about it.

I can assure you that I have experienced all of these spiritual symptoms, over and over. Until the Lord came to my rescue, I have to be honest: My prayer life was discouraging, frustrating, and defeating.

What changed? Somewhere in the middle of one of those many discouraging times, God showed me something so straightforward and uncomplicated that I could hardly believe its power. He simply said, "Come away with Me." Out of sheer desperation I obeyed, and I was amazed at the results. After my first eight-hour time out with God, I began regularly to go away with Him for short one- or two-night vacations—usually 24 to 40 hours. The result of these times away with Him have been a revitalized prayer life, refreshed body and soul, and restored and deepened intimacy with Him. I've benefited so richly that I've become a huge advocate for taking extended time to pray. I enjoy inviting others to learn the joy and rewards of "wasting time with God" as someone has aptly called it.

But wait a minute, I can hear you protesting. *You do not understand my schedule!*

I know. Trust me, I'm busy, too. It's probably fair to say that the majority of believers feel pressed for time. For most of us the idea of a "prayer retreat" sounds like a luxury we cannot afford. We say, "A day alone with God sounds *wonderful,* but I can't do it because I've got meetings and appointments and projects and commitments and responsibilities."

We don't need a retreat to pray, after all. We manage to squeeze in a quiet time most days, we go to our prayer group meetings, and we're learning to pray throughout the day—in the shower, at traffic lights, while waiting in line at the ATM. We're already praying, so why do we need—how can we justify—an entire day in prayer? Finding that kind of time is impossible! Or so it seems.

Jesus Was Busy, Too

I'm pretty sure Jesus looks at our needs, priorities, and schedules differently. No one can argue about having more demands on his time than Jesus. Yet to Him, it was impossible *not* to spend extended time with the Father. Luke tell us that Jesus frequently took extended time alone with His Father.

Jesus often withdrew to lonely places and prayed. (Lk. 5:16)

Jesus went out to a mountainside to pray, and spent the night praying to God. (Lk. 6:12)

Each day Jesus was teaching at the temple, and each evening he went out to spend the night on the hill called the Mount of Olives. (Lk. 21:37)

Jesus went out as usual to the Mount of Olives, and his disciples followed him. On reaching the place, he said to them, "Pray . . . ." (Lk. 22:39-40)

When we read between the lines of Scripture, we see that Jesus had to protect that time and make it a priority, just as we do. Mark gives us just a glimpse of how hard it was sometimes: "Very early in the morning, while it was still dark, Jesus got up, left the house and went off to a solitary place, where he prayed. Simon and his companions went to look for him, and when they found him, they exclaimed: 'Everyone is looking for you!'" (Mk. 1:35-37). (Sound familiar?)

Nevertheless, Jesus *did* make time alone with God a priority and taught His disciples to do the same. Later in Mark, we see Him addressing His ministry-weary friends. "The apostles gathered around Jesus and reported to him all they had done and taught. Then, because so many people were coming and going that they did not even have a chance to eat, he said to them, 'Come with me by yourselves to a quiet place and get some rest.' So they went away by themselves in a boat to a solitary place" (Mk. 6:30-32).

A SPIRITUAL NECESSITY

"Come away with Me." The invitation extends every bit as much to us living in the 21st century as it did to those 1st century disciples. But if prayer retreats are to be part of our lives, like Jesus and His followers then, we'll need to be intentional about it. It might mean taking a day off work or out of our weekend. It may mean hiring a babysitter. Some churches and ministries give or even require their staff to take a day off with God. Husbands can watch the kids so their wives can get away. Friends can help each other by offering their home, cabin, or condo for a retreat location. I've learned that when I make retreating with God a priority, He works out the logistics.

I'm praying that the Restorer of Souls who invites the weary and heavy burdened to come to Him for rest, will also help you to receive His gracious invitation. The refreshment He offers is not a luxury; it's a most compassionate gift and a spiritual necessity.

My soul cries out for extended time alone with God my Father and Jesus my Friend. Doesn't yours? Will you accept His invitation to come away with Him so He can refresh and restore you, and through you, others?

Chapter 2

THE BENEFITS OF
"WASTING TIME WITH GOD"

M y first time of extended prayer was a gift from a friend. I didn't even know I needed it. I was the stay-at-home mother of a busy toddler who consistently got up before 6 a.m. Scheduling even a few minutes of "adult conversation" with God demanded all my powers of creativity and perseverance. One day I must have looked a little more wild-eyed than usual because my friend announced, "You need some time alone with God. I'm coming to your house next Tuesday to watch your son. You go to my house and just be alone with the Lord. Take as long as you need."

Back then, I didn't know anyone who spent more than a half hour or so of daily quiet time with the Lord. So I wasn't sure what to do with all that time. But with no agenda in mind, I went to my friend's house, knelt in her living room, and began pouring my heart out to the Lord. As I opened my Bible, He spoke to me, and before I knew it, we'd enjoyed several hours together. He refreshed me, gave me new direction, and introduced me to the rich blessings of spending prolonged time with Him.

Your circumstances may be entirely different than the ones I just described. You may have a demanding job; a busy, growing family; or an all-consuming ministry. You may be caring for an elderly parent or a disabled child or spouse. Whatever season of life you're in, you're probably busy. Most of us are. Nevertheless, we all need these special times with God.

Since my first prayer retreat nearly two decades ago, I've spent countless days alone with the Lord in prayer, and not only when life seemed out of control and crazy. Over the years, I've discovered many more reasons we all need to enjoy extended, quality time with God. One of these is maintaining our spiritual health so we can stay in the race without burning out.

AVOIDING SPIRITUAL BURNOUT

Most of us start our Christian lives full of vision, passion, and energy. Sure we've heard stories of burnt-out pastors, missionaries, and other ministry leaders — or on the domestic front, burnt-out spouses, moms, and dads. But that won't happen to us . . . will it? Can we protect ourselves from becoming the next burnout victims? With God's help, we can. For me, the answer has been a simple preemptive measure: regular extended time with the Lord.

When I assumed the leadership of *Pray!* magazine, I had already enjoyed occasional personal prayer retreats. But I knew that the requirements of this position combined with my responsibilities to care for my disabled husband and a homeschooled teenage son would stretch me beyond anything I'd ever experienced before. So I asked my publisher if I might have one day each month off for prayer as part of my job description. He kindly agreed.

Those days set apart for God alone have been my lifeline. During these times God has shown up and kept me sane (well, *mostly* sane!). He's helped me keep my vows of "for better or worse, in sickness or in health." He's kept me creative and productive in leadership. He's refreshed me physically, spiritually, mentally, and emotionally when I was running on empty. He's helped me heal and forgive from the bumps and bruises of life. God has met me on those days in ways no one and nothing else could.

Pastor Jack Hayford says that times of solitude and waiting on the Lord are the "hallmark of people who walk steadfastly with the Lord—people who experience trials and come through with faithfulness, stability, and strength of character." How does this work? For one thing, it is during our alone times with God that we really get to know Him for who He is. We share our hearts with Him and recognize how well He knows us. We become intimate with Him in ways that build our confidence in Him so we can really trust Him and become steadfast.

NURTURING INTIMACY WITH GOD

If you're reading this book, it's entirely possible that you already have a healthy prayer life. You probably have an established time for daily prayer. You also may have learned to talk to the Lord throughout the day as you encounter challenges or remember people in need. These daily prayer habits are indispensable to our relationship with God, and they are essential to good communication. However, by themselves, they usually are not enough to cultivate the intimacy with God that we desire and need.

Our relationship with God depends on our communication with Him—not just quality, but also quantity. In that aspect, it's not much different from any other close relationship.

Early in my marriage, I realized that good communication doesn't happen automatically. Of course my husband and I *talked*. Every day David and I discussed routine domestic information such as who would take the car for the oil change or what needed to be picked up at the supermarket. But those quickie conversations on the way out the door or over a brief phone call at work didn't do much to deepen our friendship.

Happily, our communication consisted of more than just two-minute check-ins with each other. In addition to those little snatches of talk during the day, we almost always shared dinner together, which allowed regular, more leisurely times to converse. Over our evening meal we discussed the stuff of our days—problems at work, projects on the house, and commitments at church or our son's school. It was good. They were important conversations. But even those dinner talks were not enough to cultivate the intimacy we both desired.

Eventually, David and I realized that if we were going to have the kind of relationship we really wanted, we would have to carve out time to nurture it. So we started going away by ourselves for weekends and short vacations. These getaways were different from the family vacation that included our son and lots of activity. They were special times for us to relax and give each other the gift of undivided attention. It was during those times that we really got to know one another as we listened to each other's hopes, dreams, joys, fears, and disappointments.

It's the same way with our relationship with God. We need to pursue both quantity and quality conversations with Him. Our quickie prayers and calls for help throughout the day are important. So are our longer times of fellowship during our regular prayer times when we discuss problems, challenges, and commitments. But for most of us, it's during "vacations with God"—a time of extended prayer—that we really get to know Him, hear His heart, and become intimate with Him. It's been during times like those that I've learned to hear and trust His voice, which has been critical to my being able to know His will for my life.

Learning to Hear God's Counsel

Most of us very much want to know God's will for our lives. God's Word gives us general principles to follow concerning relationships and conduct. However, when it comes to specifics such as whether to serve in a certain ministry, how best to respond to a child's disobedience, what we should do about the problems we observe at church, and so on, by itself, the Bible does not give the direct counsel we long to hear. We need the Holy Spirit for that. We must learn to seek God and recognize His voice.

Early in my Christian walk I wanted to know God's will for specific, significant areas of my life that Scripture did not directly address. I knew

that He promised to give me wisdom when I lacked it (Jas. 1:5). So, I made it a habit to ask Him about these things in my daily prayer times. I believe God did honor my prayers and guided me through nudges, promptings, open and closed doors, and so on. But deep down, I also knew there could be more than that. Our God is a relational God. I wanted to talk important matters over with Him in a personal way and have Him counsel me as a loving Father. I now realize that I wasn't hearing His voice in the way I longed to, partly because of my inexperience in listening, partly because I didn't give Him enough time to speak.

I'm sure it's possible to learn to listen to God without going away on a prayer retreat. However, for me, I needed the extra focused time to learn to hear from Him. Having the luxury of uninterrupted time allowed me the opportunity to experiment with different prayer tools, such as *lectio divina* (see p. 87), dialoguing with God, meditating on God's Word and character, journaling, and so on. And over time, I learned to hear His voice more clearly and consistently.

I'm sure there are many more reasons to accept the Lord's invitation to "waste time" with Him. But there's one more significant one I want to point out: Prayer retreats allow us time for the Holy Spirit to fill us up so that we have something to offer others.

Ministering from the Overflow

Have you ever tried to deliver a life-changing talk, pray a heart-healing prayer, or speak words of compassion and comfort when you're depleted yourself? I sure have, and it's usually not very pretty. But that's not what God intends for us. He intends to be our Source, refreshing us so we in turn can refresh others.

Jesus said that we speak out of the overflow of our hearts (Lk. 6:45). Through His Spirit, He wants to enable us to be streams in the desert for those around us who are parched (Is. 32:2).

During extended time alone with God, the Holy Spirit fills me with a deeper appreciation of the Father's love and an expanded understanding of His truth. I cannot recount how many times the Lord has almost immediately called on me to share these truths with people around me. On my own I would never know how to respond to their hurts, confusion, or questions. But in the most wonderful way, God gives me exactly what I'll need to give to the people He's already planned to put in my path. When I'm called upon to teach or write, it's the same way. Most often God gives me in advance—in my own private time with Him—just what I'll need to share with those to whom He's calling me to minister. This has been one of the most amazing benefits of prayer retreats. I really start to experience the truth He promised in Jn. 7:37-38 that when we come to Him to drink, streams of living water then flow out of us and into other people.

The practice of taking prayer retreats has changed my relationship with God and with others. I cannot imagine living without the many benefits I have experienced at God's feet. And the really wonderful thing is, what God and I share during leisurely times alone is starting to spill over into my daily prayer times, too. Although it's still easiest for me to hear and receive from the Lord when I have the extended time alone with Him, I'm discovering that the truths and skills I've learned during those times help me tap into His love, guidance, and help whenever I talk to Him. And perhaps that's the greatest benefit of all.

Others have experienced the rich benefits of "wasting time with God." Here are some of their stories.

WHY A DAY OF PRAYER?
by Lorne Sanny

Why take this time from a busy life? What is it for?

For extended fellowship with God beyond your morning devotions. It means just plain being with and thinking about God. God has called us into the fellowship of his Son, Jesus Christ (1 Cor. 1:9). Like many personal relationships, this fellowship is nurtured by spending time together. God takes special note of times when His people revere Him and think upon His name (see Mal. 3:16).

For a renewed perspective. Like flying over the battlefield in a reconnaissance plane, a day of prayer gives us the opportunity to think of the world from God's point of view. Especially when going through times of difficulty we need this perspective to sharpen our vision of the unseen and to let the immediate, tangible things drop into proper place. Our spiritual defenses are strengthened while "we fix our eyes not on what is seen, but on what is unseen. For . . . what is unseen is eternal" (2 Cor. 4:18).

For catching up on intercession. There are nonChristian friends and relatives to bring before the Lord, missionaries, our pastors, our neighbors and Christian associates, our government leaders—to name a few.

For prayerful consideration of our own lives before the Lord. You will especially want to spend a day in prayer when facing important decisions, as well as on a periodic basis. On such a day you can evaluate where you are in relation to your goals and get direction from the Lord through His Word. Promises are there for you and me, just as they have been for Hudson Taylor or George Müeller or Dawson Trotman. And it is in our times alone with God that He gives inner assurance of His promises to us.

For adequate preparation. The first two chapters of Nehemiah describe the launching of Nehemiah's plans for rebuilding the wall of Jerusalem. In Neh. 2:12 he speaks of "what my God had put in my heart to do for Jerusalem." When had God put this plan in his heart? I believe it was during the time mentioned in the opening verses of this book, in which Nehemiah spent "some days" (v. 4) in prayer before the God of heaven. He fasted and prayed and waited on God, and when the day for action came, he was ready.[1]

A PLACE OF TRANSFORMATION
by Gary Skinner

It all began 10 years ago. On the floor. On my face. I was lying with my arms up over my head and my nose planted firmly in the carpet.

"Well, Lord, I was told today at church that if I would get on my face and worship You, I could find some answers . . . that I could connect with You . . . that You would change me. Is this what they meant?"

My nose was beginning to get a little rug burned so I turned my head and let my cheek rest on the floor. I continued to lay there for almost two hours. You see, I was desperate. My history was more than a little embarrassing. I was 40 years old and here's what I had to show for it: a divorce, a bankruptcy, a lost business, $500,000 of debt, and the prestige of being a convicted felon. It's true that I now was married to a wonderful woman and had some great friends. But the shame of my past still dominated my thoughts.

My list of atrocities did not happen overnight. I strung them out over a 22-year period. What's interesting is that during those years I consistently read my Bible, went to church or Bible studies, prayed, and openly spoke about my love for and commitment to God. Yet I was a mess. A terrible disciple of Jesus Christ. So, in many ways, lying on my face that day was a "retreat." I had retreated into God's presence to lay down my old life – and, hopefully, emerge with something new.

I was looking for something spectacular. You know, an audible voice, a visitation from Jesus, or even a glimpse of an angel. But I got nothing. Yet as I continued to pour out my heart to God and wait, I knew deep within that I was on the right track. Finally, I prayed, *Lord, I know a lot about You. But I don't think I know You. Something is missing. Will You teach me about You? Will You change me? Will You rewire the way I think? I'm really tired of living life my way.*

That was all it took. I became overwhelmingly aware of God's presence. I decided that these "floor retreats" were a good thing. So for the next eight months, I began to meet with God in the same room, on the same floor, in the same position, three to four nights a week — for sometimes up to three hours — while the Holy Spirit gently taught, corrected, and transformed my life. What started out as an experiment turned into a discipline. Eventually, it became a lifestyle.

Retreat Advances

Over the next three years, everything changed. In every area of my life where I had produced failure, success moved in. No, I didn't become perfect, but my wife and others who knew me well began to comment that something was "different" about Gary.

I want to make a couple of things clear, however. One is that not all of my "floor retreats" were amazing encounters with God. Sometimes I finished a session and wondered if I had wasted my time. Sometimes I fell asleep. Sometimes my prayers seemed to go only about three inches off the floor, and God seemed a million miles away. Other times, however, His presence was overpowering. I remember moments when I felt I was glued to the floor. Or times when I would lie there with tears streaming down my face, but I didn't sense that I was overly happy or sad. It was more like a cleansing. On one occasion, I thought for sure I could feel God *breathing* on me.

The second thing I want to mention is that my transformation was gradual. I'm not saying it always has to be, but that's how it worked out in my life.

One morning after I had been meeting with God for about three weeks, I woke up and thought, *I don't know if this is doing anything at all. I don't think I'm really changing.* Later that day somebody on the freeway cut me off and almost forced me into a ditch. I immediately responded, *Lord, bless that guy. He probably feels awful that he did that. He's probably going through something difficult and his mind wasn't on his driving.*

I drove for another two miles and then it hit me: *Who was that? That's not how the Gary Skinner I know would normally handle himself!* Hmmm. It was clear that God had been up to something all those hours while I was on my face on the floor.

Sharing the Floor with Others

During my three years of change, I had the privilege of becoming an associate pastor at the church I was attending. In light of my past, this in itself was a miracle. When I was asked to interview for the position, I thought for sure I would be disqualified because of my sordid past. But one of the associate pastors told me, "Gary, we've been watching your life over the last couple of years and some of us who know you believe you would be perfect for this position. You have been transformed."

As time passed, my "floor retreats" became something of a trademark for me. Some people might have thought they were a gimmick. Others might have thought they were foolish. All I know is that they worked. I think they worked because they brought me face-to-face with God, who knew exactly what I needed for true transformation — and He can perform life-changes in a way that no human counselor or program can.

A couple of years ago, I was meeting with a friend who was sincerely hungry for change. I explained what I had learned from my floor retreats about humility and honesty before God. He decided to put it to the test. When we met about a week and a half later, he said, "I've been getting up early every morning, lying on the floor, and waiting on the Lord. Nothing is happening. Any advice?"

"Yes," I said. "Keep doing it. If nothing has happened a few months from now, let's talk."

I know that wasn't what he was hoping for. I know he was hoping there was a shortcut somewhere. Maybe there is. But I don't know what it is. The good news is that it didn't take that long for my friend. In fact, within three weeks he had an incredible testimony of how God was speaking to him and directing his steps.[2]

Chapter 3

WHAT TO EXPECT FROM A PRAYER RETREAT

S ometimes when I mention prayer retreats I get dubious stares. "I could never spend a *whole day* praying!" some people object. But as we talk more about it, I usually discover that they are imagining a prayer retreat as something a whole lot more intimidating than what I'm actually inviting them to.

WHAT A PRAYER RETREAT IS *NOT*

The problem often is rooted in how many of us define prayer. Many of us think of it primarily as a verbal sharing of needs and requests with God. According to this definition, we think about the needs we, our families, friends, church, city, and nation have and then recite them to God, asking for His intervention. Certainly this kind of praying — known as "petition" or "supplication" — is prayer. It's an incredibly important kind of prayer that God invites us to use regularly. But the idea of spending hours listing problems, failures, shortages, illnesses, heartaches, challenges, and worries sounds boring at best and depressing at worst. And that's just *our* side of it. If that were our only conversation with Him for an entire day, I suspect even God might find it a little wearisome. Prayer retreats are not just about petition.

Christians who have been praying for a while usually recognize that in addition to petition, prayer also includes worship, praise, confession, and thanksgiving. Some of us use prayer models like the Lord's Prayer from Matthew 6 or the ACTS acronym (adoration, confession, thanksgiving, and supplication) to ensure that our prayer includes more than just requests and to bring balance to our prayer times. Like petition, these different kinds of prayer conversations are very important, and the Lord invites us, even commands us, to have them.

Certainly, prayer that includes these varied conversations can keep most of us involved a lot longer than pure petition could. However, these kinds of prayer are nevertheless limited in that they are all one-sided, *verbal* prayer. In each of them, it's up to us to carry the conversation and God's job is merely to listen. I venture to say that even the most talkative among us would say that keeping up a nonstop conversation for an entire day would be a daunting task. For that reason I'm glad that prayer retreats are not just about verbal prayer.

On the other hand, there's an entirely different category of people I meet who at first are not the least bit daunted by the idea of prayer retreats. It's not necessarily that they have prayer all figured out or have logged years of prayer retreats. Rather, some folks use the term "prayer retreat" more loosely, more in the sense of a *spiritual* retreat or "God Time" than a retreat focused entirely on prayer. These good people broaden their retreat times to include things like Bible study, reading Christian books and magazines, and exploring nature. These are all good activities and may very well warrant spending a day away to engage in them from time to time. However, strictly speaking, prayer retreats are not times to catch up on Bible study or sermon preparation. Nor are they occasions to spend hours of uninterrupted time reading Christian books (no, not even material on prayer!). And while it's certainly true that on a prayer retreat we may take some walks in nature, prayer retreats are not generally intended to be times in which we focus our attention on hiking and watching wildlife.

WHAT TO EXPECT FROM A PRAYER RETREAT

What a Prayer Retreat Is

So what is a prayer retreat, then? Obviously the definition will vary from person to person and no one definition is the "right" one. However, after many years of trial and error, I'd suggest that an effective prayer retreat usually includes the following significant components.

Time with God, not just about Him

First we want to keep the purpose of our prayer retreat very intentionally in mind. We are setting aside this time so we can deepen our relationship with God. We do this as we focus exclusively on listening to God and expressing our hearts to Him. When we keep this focus in mind, we will not merely think about, read about, watch DVDs about, listen to music about, or talk *about* God. Our time will be a *with* not an *about* time. So we will aim to include God in every thought, word, song, or act. Everything we do during our time will include a mindfulness of His presence and attention to us. We will learn new ways of hearing Him as well as new ways of speaking to Him. But no matter what form our communication takes, we will be interacting *with* God.

Creative expression

It has been fun for me to discover some of the variety of ways God invites us to interact with Him. On my first prayer retreat years ago, I hadn't experimented with prayer much, so my prayer was limited to what I could verbalize to God and what I could hear from Him from His Word. But over the years I've learned that those are just two ways we interact with Him. There are so many more just waiting to be discovered.

As we know, in many ways our relationship with God corresponds to the ways we relate to close friends and family members. For example, lovers use more than just *talk* to share with each other. They can communicate volumes with a touch, a look, a special gift, an inside joke, a note, or even a simple act like doing the dishes or cooking a favorite meal. Similarly, during prayer retreats, we learn ways of communicating with God that go far beyond spoken words.

We can consciously cultivate a spirit of adventure during our prayer retreats, using the time as an opportunity to try prayer experiments. Sometimes we might try things that go outside our comfort zone (for example, see the next chapter for times I've danced with God!). Other times we may try prayer approaches we've heard about from other believers.

Direction by God

Our time with God is a time *for* God. He enjoys our company and longs for extended time with us even more than we long to share it with Him. Revelation 3:20 paints a poignant picture of our Lord standing outside the doors of His children's hearts, knocking, hoping, and yearning for us to open up to Him so He can come in and fellowship with us. So we want to remember that this time is not primarily about us.

During our prayer retreats, God will meet and satisfy us as we focus on Him. But having our needs met should not be the main goal for our prayer retreat. First of all, He knows our needs better than we do; besides that He has things on His mind that He wants to share with us, if only we'll take time to listen.

For these reasons, I try to hold loosely to any agenda I might have for my prayer retreats. That doesn't mean I avoid making plans for what I'd like to do with God. For example, I usually begin my retreats with specific ideas of what I'd like to talk with Him about, such as a ministry responsibility for which I need inspiration, a difficulty for which I need insight, or a disappointment or loss for which I need hope and comfort. However, at the beginning of each prayer retreat, I intentionally release my agenda to God and invite Him to direct our time together. Sometimes He wants to talk about the same things I do. Other times He surprises me and wants to do something different entirely. But whether we spend most of our time on the things I wanted to talk about or do something totally different, I can honestly say I've never been disappointed. He knows me and loves me and when I let Him steer our time together, it is always good.

Uninterrupted time

Each component of an effective prayer retreat requires solitude and a generous amount of uninterrupted time. Ideally, I plan to go away for my prayer retreats. That's because whenever I've tried to retreat at home I've been too distracted by the phone, doorbell, Internet, and the myriad tasks that scream for my attention. So I try to go to a quiet place where none of these things will distract me.

The ideal timeframe will vary from person to person. What works best for me is to settle into my prayer retreat place at about 5 p.m., just after work. I try to spend two nights, leaving at about 8 a.m. on the last day, for a total of about 40 hours. That's my ideal. The truth is, however, that life is not always ideal. More often, my prayer retreats last 24 hours. I try to include an overnight stay because I find that I am more able to get real rest and refreshing when I go to sleep and wake up focused on God. But sometimes I cannot manage even 24 hours away. When I can't arrange to have a prayer retreat any other way, I take an eight-hour retreat, from 8 a.m. to 4 p.m. When we give God our undivided attention, even eight hours can accomplish great things.

WHAT SHOULD I EXPECT FROM A PRAYER RETREAT?

The Lord rewards us when we spend with Him. But how He does so is up to Him. In my experience, sometimes it's been a fresh encounter with His love. Sometimes He gives me counsel for a decision. Sometimes God shares His perspective on a trial that helps me to endure. Occasionally I enjoy a breakthrough in a personal struggle or in my intercession for a loved one. Often He gives me words or ways to encourage someone else. Almost always I feel a release from my burdens. As I experiment with new and creative ways of connecting with Him, I sometimes find a prayer practice that carries over into my daily prayer life.

I have never left a retreat without in some way enjoying God's very personal encouragement. Sometimes He gives it in ways I had expected, sometimes it's in different ways entirely. I don't always have a shivers-up-the-spine encounter with Him. In fact, I usually don't. I don't always get the specific direction or answers I'd hoped to get. I don't always spend time interceding for people the way I thought I would. But no matter what happens—or doesn't—I am always glad I spent the time with Him.

However, some things always happen on every prayer retreat for me. These include

- physical rest
- change of scenery
- freedom from the clock and external demands on time
- time out from stress, worry, and pressures
- pleasing God

God promises specific benefits for people who take the time to wait on Him. So no matter what actually happens on our retreats, extended time with God is always time well spent. Lamentations 3:25-26 says that "The LORD is good to those whose hope is in him, to the one who seeks him; it is good to wait quietly for the salvation of the LORD." And Is. 40:31 promises that "those who hope in the LORD will renew their strength. They will soar on wings like eagles; they will run and not grow weary, they will walk and not be faint."

There is nothing like a prayer retreat to cultivate this quality of waiting on the Lord. And we can be sure He will meet us when we do. *But what will we do with all this time alone with God?* you may still be wondering. The answer is, *lots* of things.

Chapter 4

WHAT TO DO ON YOUR
PRAYER RETREAT

Okay, we're finally to the point where we can address the most commonly asked question about prayer retreats: How will I spend all that time?

Keeping in mind that prayer retreats involve a whole lot more than petition or even our words spoken to God (see chapter 3), you can enjoy your special time with God in many ways, more than you will possibly be able to explore in just one retreat.

What follows is a collection of ideas and options that is by no means comprehensive. As you and the Lord grow deeper in your relationship, the two of you will explore new ideas not even mentioned here. But to get started, read through these suggestions, and ask the Lord which ones He might like you to experiment with during your next extended time with Him. Then trust Him to guide you. Usually certain ones will seem to jump out to you; these are probably the ones you should try first.

Some of these ideas may not seem like prayer to you, but praise and worship are part of prayer. Hearing from God is the other side of prayer, God's response to us. Lifting our hearts to Him in silent meditation and wonder is prayer. So allow the Holy Spirit to stretch you as He leads you into new ways to communicate with your Father.

Think of these ideas as a buffet from which you can choose as many or as few ideas as you like. Do not feel that you should attempt all of them in a single retreat. If you do only one of them and God meets you there, great! The goal is to find a means to connect with the Lord so you can get to know Him better.

MAKE MUSIC

There's something about music that helps me to open up to the Lord and receive from Him more readily. If that's also true for you, you may want to employ music in your prayer retreat.

- Take along a hymn or worship-chorus book so you can sing to the Lord. Often when I'm meditating on Him, a song comes to mind. For example, recently I was thinking about what it means to clothe ourselves with Christ (Gal. 3:27). As I pondered the idea, the hymn "The Solid Rock" came to mind, especially the part about being "clothed in His righteousness alone, faultless to stand before the throne." So I looked up the hymn and sang it to the Lord. I don't have a solo voice. I wouldn't sing for you! But I enjoy singing to God, and I think He enjoys it, too.
- Bring along some worship music, in whatever form works best for you: CD, tape, MP3, etc. I like to have my music as portable as possible so I can take it along with me on a walk with God. I can worship Him anywhere, but it's sometimes especially meaningful for me to sing His praises while I'm enjoying His creation. Sometimes I also like to play worship music as I'm going to sleep on my retreats. It's nice to end the day soaking in the worship of God.
- If you play an instrument, consider bringing it along and playing for Him. I'm no concert performer, but sometimes I bring my violin on prayer retreats so I can serenade God. I select songs that express my heart for Him, and then play to an audience of One.

I picture myself as a child playing for my heavenly Father. Wrong notes and hesitating melodies don't matter to Him. He sees my heart and enjoys what I offer Him.

- Get some new music especially created for worship and intercession. Some of these recordings are instrumental while others have vocals (for example, the International House of Prayer has many vocal CDs created for intercession. Go to www.ihop.org/Shop to look at some of them. I prefer instrumental music because words usually distract me. "Come to the Waters" (http://phxgolf.com/wvap-00001.html) is a creative instrumental CD I've enjoyed. The tunes are unfamiliar so I can't sing along even if I wanted to — unless I make up my own prayer words, which I've sometimes done. Also Wes and Stacy Campbell have a series of CDs that provide music intended to be used when you pray certain passages of Scripture such as Psalms, Song of Solomon, and Revelation (http://shop. newdayinternational.org/customer/home.php?cat=95&page=2).

MEDITATE

Joshua 1:8 commands us to meditate on God's Word day and night (see also Ps. 1:2, 119:97). If we're honest, most of us really don't even come close to meditating that constantly, if we meditate at all. But a prayer retreat — when we literally do have at least one day and night just for God — is a prime opportunity to start learning this delightful prayer practice.

The Old Testament word for *meditate* suggests "muttering" or "musing." It is a leisurely process in which we take a verse or characteristic of God or His creation and chew on it, turning it over in our hearts and minds and inviting the Holy Spirit to let the truths and graces of God root deeply in us.

The psalmists mention meditation at least 16 times, urging the faithful to meditate on God's laws, unfailing love, mighty deeds, precepts, ways, decrees, wonders, statutes, promises, things done by His hands, and wonderful works (1:2; 48:9; 77:12; 119:15,23,27,78,99,148; 143:5; 145:5). We can meditate on a single word of Scripture, a verse, or an entire passage. We can choose an aspect of God's character, such as His patience or justice, and ponder that deeply.

Perhaps the Holy Spirit will invite us to meditate on a particular promise of God, as it applies to our lives at the moment. We may take a walk in nature and mediate on God's works. We may be led to mull over an aspect of Jesus' life and ministry, such as His incarnation, sacrifice, or resurrection. We may want to take time with one of the metaphors for Christ, such as Good Shepherd, Bread of Life, or Light of the World. Or, we can contemplate God's work and grace in our lives. What we meditate on will be different on different retreats, but it's a good idea to spend a significant amount of time in quiet contemplation. The following are several kinds of meditation you may want to try.

- Take a walk with God and notice His creation. Look for both big and small, living and inanimate. Take time to notice details. Talk to God about what you see.
- Ask the Lord to refresh you both spiritually and physically. Prayerfully select Scripture from the following list to meditate on: Ps. 23:2-3, 62:1-5, 91:1; Prov. 11:25; Is. 30:15; Mt. 11:28-29; Acts. 3:19; Heb. 4:1-11.
- Select a short, familiar passage such as Psalm 23, Isaiah 53, Mt. 5:3-12 or 6:9-13. Ask the Holy Spirit to make the passage come alive. Then read it out loud slowly, concentrating on each word. Wait in silence for several minutes, allowing the words to settle in your mind and heart. Repeat this process at least two more times, being careful not to rush. Don't try to "figure out" what the passage means. Instead, let the Lord speak to your heart with it. Write down your thoughts and questions and talk to the Lord about them.
- Choose an attribute of God (e.g. patience, mercy, justice, love),

a description of Jesus (our great High Priest, Friend of sinners, King of kings, etc.), or an aspect of Christ's work (e.g. atonement, intercessor between God and men, reconciler) and invite Him to reveal Himself to you in that trait. Listen for Him. He may bring a Scripture to mind, an event or issue in your life, an example of His work in someone else's life, an image or word picture, or any other means to help you better see and appreciate this trait of His. Again, take your time. Do not force or rush this process. It isn't a Bible study or an intellectual challenge — it's quiet receiving from the Lord as You open yourself to Him.

USE WORDS

Even the kind of prayer we are most familiar with, verbal prayer, has many variations. Use your prayer retreat as an opportunity to experiment with new styles of prayer or to just enjoy uninterrupted time with the ones you already appreciate. Here are some possibilities.

- Pray some of the great prayers of all time — start with a psalm or a book of time-tested prayers such as John Baille's *A Diary of Private Prayer* or *The Book of Common Prayer.*
- With the Holy Spirit's help, spend time in extended intercession for those for whom you have committed to pray.
- Thank the Lord for everything you can think of. Write down each blessing as you pray it. Take your time. Think of what God has given you and done for you both spiritually and materially.
- Pray the Lord's Prayer, lingering over each phrase and personalizing it according to where you are in life at the moment.

Practice Listening and Interactive Prayer

I learned to hear from God on prayer retreats. I didn't learn it all at once, but on each prayer retreat, I would experiment with listening techniques (such as journaling, *lectio divina* [see p. 87], and dialoguing), wait with my spiritual ears open, test what I heard, and grow in confidence that God really was speaking to me.

Many books and articles are available on listening prayer, and you should by all means use whatever ones are helpful to you. But the main thing to remember is that God does speak to His children. His sheep know His voice (Jn. 10:3). If hearing from God is new to you, ask Him to speak. Ask Him to teach you how to listen for Him and trust His voice. And be patient with the process. Here are some things you can try to prime the pump.

- Write a letter to God, starting with "Dear Father." Tell Him how much you love and appreciate Him. Then on a new page or sheet of paper, write "Dear (insert your own name)," and write down what you think He is saying to you.
- Choose a passage of Scripture that you'd like to interact with God on. Read it, and then talk to Him about your questions, reservations, struggles, or hopes regarding that passage. Quietly wait for His response. Write it down. Keep the dialogue going. After He's spoken to you, respond to Him with your appreciation, further questions, and so on. Speak to Him in normal conversation and remember not to monopolize.
- Dialogue with the Lord about a specific burden. Ask Him for wisdom, comfort, perspective, direction, correction, or help. Listen for Him and write down what you think you hear Him saying. Be aware that He will want to speak to you as a Father talks to His child. Don't be all business in your listening; listen for His affection and heart for you, too.
- Ask God what *He* would like to talk to you about, then just listen. After you've heard His heart, respond to Him with yours.

Try Guided Prayer

As we've already discussed, a prayer retreat is not a time to catch up on our reading, even good reading like the Bible or spiritual books. However, we may want to let small bits of Scripture or prayer classics act as springboards for our praying. Here are some suggestions.

- Prayerfully and meditatively read a short book from the Bible such as Ephesians, Philippians, James, or 1 John. Read a few verses, and then talk to God about what you read. Then read some more. Continue the process until you finish the book. If the book includes any prayers in it, personalize them and pray them for yourself and for others the Holy Spirit brings to mind.
- Read a short portion of a devotional classic on prayer or the Christian life. Writings by Oswald Chambers, Andrew Murray, or A. W. Tozer are possibilities. Pay attention to whether the Holy Spirit tugs at your heart or convicts you. Talk to the Lord about these feelings and desires.
- For a guided worship experience, you might try worshiping along to "I Am: 365 Names of God" by John Paul Jackson. This powerful CD features the narration of 365 names, attributes, and characteristics of God over a powerful musical backdrop.
- If you've recently read an article about prayer that challenged you, bring it along with you and spend time praying through it with the Lord. Ask Him whether this is a prayer practice or attitude He wants you to adopt, and if so, ask Him to help you. Begin practicing.
- Use a map to help you pray for the nations of the world. Let the Holy Spirit guide you as you take your time to pray for missionaries, friends, political situations, natural disasters, and so on.

Get Physical

Sometimes I find it easier to connect with God when I involve my body in my praying. We're told to love the Lord with our hearts, souls, minds, and *strength*, so I'm pretty sure the Lord enjoys our making prayer a holistic experience that engages our hearts, minds, and bodies. Try some of these ideas to get you started.

- Try a new prayer posture. Sitting in a chair or lying in bed, while common prayer postures for us, are not the ones most commonly mentioned in Scripture. There's nothing wrong with those prayer postures, but there's something about kneeling, raising our hands, or even lying prostrate that engages our hearts more deeply in prayer (Phil. 2:10; 1 Tim. 2:8; Mt. 26:39).
- Prayerwalk the neighborhood. As you go, ask the Holy Spirit to help you know how to pray. Notice houses, businesses, vacant lots, troubled areas, and intercede for them. You may be the first person ever to pray for some of the people who live and work there.
- Dance before the Lord. David did it (2 Sam. 6:14), and so can we! In fact, did you know Scripture virtually commands it? Psalm 149:3 says, "Let them praise his name with dancing." I haven't danced in public since my Jewish friend's wedding in about 1990. But I sometimes dance on my prayer retreats, even though it's far out of my comfort zone. I put on some music, fast or contemplative, depending on my mood, close the blinds so no one but God can see me, and go at it.

   How is this prayer, you may ask? I think of it as expressing my heart to God through movement. He knows my dancing is for Him. I wouldn't do if for anyone else. As I dance I think of the freedom He gives me and the joy I have in His presence and the future dancing we'll all be doing at the Wedding Feast. My heart is lifted to Him.

- Take communion. Read the story of the last supper (Lk. 22:14-20), and meditate on the Lord's body and blood and what each purchased for you. Talk to Jesus about it. Then participate with Him by taking bread and wine or grape juice in remembrance of Him. Thank Him. Receive His love for you in a fresh way.
- At the end of your prayer retreat, make notes or journal about what was most significant or enjoyable about what you and God have shared together. Keep these notes to reflect on at future prayer retreats.

These are ways I've enjoyed my prayer retreat times. In the next few pages you'll read the experiences of others who have cultivated a lifestyle of extended prayer times. And this is just the tip of the iceberg when it comes to how you can spend your time with the Lord. He will give you more as you continue to get away with Him.

DISCOVER THE DELIGHT OF A DAY ALONE WITH GOD
by Richard LaFountain

My first experience with a full day of prayer was awful.

Like so many wannabe prayer warriors, I was under the impression that prayer was talking at God, telling Him everything He needed to fix in the world. But that kind of "prayer" is exhausting, and, to tell the truth, it's not much fun.

I approached that first day loaded with lists of prayer requests: for my church, our national missions organization, my personal concerns. Within two hours, my batteries died and my mind wandered. Finally, I awoke, drooling all over my Bible.

I had run through all my lists and added a few hundred spontaneous things as well. *Now what? What does one pray when the lists are done? Do we just do it all over again? If this is what a prayer retreat is all about*, I decided, *then I am not cut out for it.*

Thankfully, God did not leave me there. He began to teach me new lessons in prayer that changed everything.

Intimacy Precedes Intercession

One of the first things God taught me was that spending extended time in prayer does not mean expanding my list of prayer requests, which are then read off to God like a shopping list. If prayer is a taste of heaven, then it should be enjoyable – and create a craving for more.

I quickly learned that when prayer is a delightful experience, extending it is never a problem. I delight in sitting by the sea and watching the waves crashing onto the shore. I delight in soaking in a hot tub when my body aches from a long day of labor. I delight in dinner and conversation with friends at a fine restaurant. No one has to force me to do these things because I delight in them. Yet none of them compares to the delight I have found in spending time alone with God.

It was not the needs of the world that drove the great men of God to their knees, I discovered. It was their God-hunger! They had tasted the Lord Himself, had found Him good, and wanted more. That's what happens when the Lord Himself – not our petitions – becomes the focus of our prayers. The delight produced by that intimacy with our heavenly Father makes us want *more*.

Being Still

My second lesson came from Ps. 46:10: "Be still, and know that I am God." How could I expect to spend extended times with God when I couldn't sit still for five minutes?

I have what I call Spiritual Attention Deficit Disorder. I am a doer, an overachiever. My to-do lists scream at me, "Pick me! Do me first!" For a while, I argued with God about how good I was at getting things done and how important it was for Him to have people with my personality type. Yet God spoke more loudly still: "In quietness and confidence shall be your strength, but you would not" (Is. 30:15, NKJV).

38

God nailed me. He put His finger on my problem: "I would not." I thought I was too busy to stay and pray. I valued my achievements more than God's commands. I loved *working* more than *waiting*.

To train me for future times of extended prayer, God directed me to an unlikely tool: a three-minute egg timer. He prompted me to use it every day until I could become quiet and still in His presence.

The Learning Curve

That first day, I lay face down on the floor with a pillow under me. I flipped the timer over and started "being still." Let me just say that three minutes is an eternity when you are not used to being still! When the timer ran out, my body had been (nearly) still for three minutes – but my mind was no quieter than when I started. So, I flipped the timer over again. Same thing. My mind was a wild stallion that refused to be dominated. For 36 minutes, I lay there, trying unsuccessfully to be still. I finally got up and told the Lord that the timer thing didn't work. *Try it again tomorrow,* He said.

I thought it was improbable that my mind would ever become still. But I tried the next day, and the next day, and the next. Each day, God taught me something new about putting away the distracting thoughts and the mental voices that clamored for my attention. It was like the process you go through in cleaning a room: picking up the clutter and putting each thing in its proper place.

Finally, the day came when I was able to clean house completely and lay quietly before the Lord. It was awesome! It was like being picked up on a cloud and carried into His presence. It was like soaking in a tub of warm water, relaxing and resting in Jesus! I found it so enjoyable I didn't want to leave.

That's when the Lord said, *OK, now you can pray.* So I moved from quiet restfulness to deep worship and adoration, to thanksgiving and blessing, to confession and clothing myself in His righteousness. Once this was accomplished, my heart poured out my own cares and then the concerns I had for others and the world.

When I finally arose from my prayer position, I was shocked to find that I had spent nearly two hours in prayer—and was nowhere near being done. I cried, *Lord, where am I going to find time to pray like this? This will take all day, or even a couple of days!*

He whispered back, *Good. Now we're ready to spend extended time together.*

Entering the Holy of Holies

God followed up by giving me a plan for ordering extended times with Him. He showed me that just as the priests of the Old Testament went through certain steps in order to enter the Holy of Holies, so I needed certain steps to enter into His presence. The Lord directed me to six. I typically take at least 45 minutes or longer on each step, viewing each one as an important part of approaching God's throne. Only after I've completed these six steps of intimacy do I find that I am finally in a place where I can intercede for my friends, my church, the world, and the lost. Here are the steps that have revolutionized my extended times of prayer:

Be still

This was the hardest—but the most helpful—thing God taught me. I still take an egg timer to my private prayer retreats. I consciously let go of "stuff" (lists of things to do, anxieties over tomorrow, etc.). Sometimes I have to write it all down, but after doing that, I literally push away the writing pad. Then I surrender my empty hands and prepared mind for God's use. Lying facedown on the floor helps me to yield completely to Him. Then I simply stay still. I just wait. I listen. I don't think. I just bask in the sunshine of God's presence.

Be worshipful

To worship is to take time to meditate on who God is in all His glory, until the truth of His greatness fills us with awe, adoration, and love. For me, this is an active step. I sing hymns and praise songs to God. I read psalms of praise to God out loud. I involve my body with shouting, bowing, clapping, dancing, lifting my hands, kneeling. Sometimes I go through the alphabet from A to Z, listing an attribute of God that begins with each letter. Or I meditate on the names of God. If I'm able to be outdoors, I take a walk with God and worship Him for His creation: I search the stars, watch a bird, stare at the waves, study a bug.

Be thankful

In this step, I recognize the hand of God and thank Him for it. I give God credit for what He has done. I thank God for His creation, including my own body (Ps. 139:14). I thank Him for His provisions. I thank God for the people He has put in my life. I thank Him for the smallest things I can think of and then work toward the bigger things. Then I thank God for the hard things—the trials and adversities that come to make me strong (1 Thess. 5:18).

Confess sin

Next, I do a spiritual inventory. Sometimes I pray through Psalm 51 or 139 to get started. Then I ask God to show me where I have sinned in my words, attitudes, thoughts, and actions. When I have confessed everything He brings to mind, I lay my sins on Jesus and appropriate His forgiveness.

Clothe yourself

Once I'm washed and clean by confession, it's time to get dressed. Romans 13:14 says to clothe ourselves with the Lord Jesus Christ, so the first part of this step is asking God to help me see myself the way He sees me. I go through a list of Scriptures and declare who I am in Christ. After this step, I pray through Eph. 6:11–18, putting on my spiritual armor. I also do spiritual warfare, resisting the devil (Jas. 4:7), claiming the blood of Jesus (Rev. 12:11), pulling down strongholds (2 Cor. 10:3–5), and erecting hedges of protection (Ezk. 22:30).

Cast your burdens

If I'm going to spend time any time during my prayer retreat to intercede for others, I find that I cannot bypass this step. Before I can pray for others, I must clear away the baggage of my own personal concerns, needs, and cares. I do this by taking my time to pray for family, finances, frustrations, fears, faults, and failures. I consciously cast all my anxiety on Him (1 Pet. 5:7) and then ask Him to help me leave it there.

As I've followed these steps, my extended prayer times have been transformed into delightful prayer days — weekends, even. They are like heavenly holidays, God-vacations, to me. It is so exciting, exhilarating, and pleasurable to get away alone with God — letting Him hold me, surround me with His love, and whisper peace to my busy heart. I long for these extended times with God. I pine for them. I plan for them.[3]

A DAY TO PRAY
by Lonni Collins Pratt

There's no telling what circumstances will compel you to set aside a day for prayer. Maybe it's a critical decision to be made, a problem to wrestle, or a call to abandon and surrender some destructive habit. You might have a growing sense that you need renewal or a day to celebrate God in your life.

I've been drawn to set aside a day of prayer for all of these reasons mentioned above. I never thought one day could make such a difference. I discover my mind is cleared, my vision keener, and my ear better tuned to the voice of God after such a day.

Of course, a day of prayer won't always change your life, and it won't always be earth moving. But, as those who have made this a regular practice will testify, it is always worthwhile.

Preparation

Since it's just a day, preparation will probably be minimal. Pick a date. Write it into your schedule, then tell someone close to you about it — a spouse, parent, pastor, or best friend. Plan to get together with that person after your day apart to discuss what happened.

The Shape of Your Day

Of course, you don't want to be tied to a rigid schedule. Yet, you don't want to spend the time daydreaming or doodling in your journal either. I've found it helpful to follow this model: Read a Bible passage prayerfully, slowly, with an open heart. Rather than reading it like a textbook or self-help book, listen to Scripture with a prayerful, yielded, open mind. It helps to read one word at a time, loud enough to hear yourself.

When something strikes a chord in you, stop reading and concentrate on that insight. Prayerfully meditate on it, allowing it to sink slowly and deeply into your spirit, paying attention to your inner, honest response. Don't rush.

From meditating on the Living Word, move to writing about your insight. You might do this as a written prayer to God or a journal-like record. This, too, should be done without hurry. If new insights come to you, repeat the process. When you are ready to continue reading, go back to Scripture and begin the process again. I like to take my readings from the gospels or epistles. Psalms are also fertile material for prayerful reading.

After doing this for two or three hours, take a break to worship and rest in God. You might select a hymn or chorus to sing. I like to pray two or three psalms also, then quietly rest in the presence of God, listening for Him to speak to my spirit.

When I feel ready for a break, I usually take a walk and have a small meal or snack. Then, I return to praying in the same way.

I reserve the last hour of my prayer day to record my feelings, what I understand has happened, and to make commitments or plans according to any discoveries God has given me.

Ending the Day

Don't think you have to come away with an extraordinary experience or blazing new insights. By being present and available to God, you will cooperate with God the best you can.

In evaluating your day, it isn't the emotional experience that matters. It isn't new insights or resolutions. If you have become fully vulnerable to God and to the transforming power of the Word of God in Scripture, it will show in your daily living.

That's why it's important to make a habit of setting apart days for prayer. The result of scheduled, frequent prayer days will be an increase in everyday prayer. Prayer, I've learned, produces a desire for prayer.[4]

HOW TO SPEND A DAY IN PRAYER
by Lorne Sanny

Perhaps you haven't spent a protracted time in prayer because you aren't sure what you would do with a whole day on your hands just to pray. Even if you have all day, you will want to use it profitably. So lose no time in starting, and start purposefully. Here's what I do.

Wait on the Lord

Divide the day into three parts: waiting on the Lord, prayer for others, and prayer for yourself. As you wait on the Lord, don't hurry. Just seek the Lord, waiting on *Him*. Isaiah 40:31 promises that those who wait upon the Lord will renew their strength. In Ps. 62:5 David says, "My soul, wait thou only upon God; for my expectation is from him."

Wait on God first to *realize His presence*. Read through a passage such as Psalm 139, grasping the truth of His presence with you as you read each verse. Ponder the impossibility of being anywhere in the universe where He is not.

Wait on him also for *cleansing*. The last two verses of Psalm 139 lead you into this. Ask God to search your heart as these verses suggest. When we search our hearts it can lead to imaginations, morbid introspection, or anything the enemy may want to throw before us. But when the Holy Spirit searches He will bring to your attention that which should be confessed and cleansed.

Psalms 51 and 32, David's songs of confession, will help you. Stand upon the firm ground of 1 Jn. 1:9 and claim God's faithfulness to forgive whatever specific thing you confess. If you realize you've sinned against another person, make a note of it so you won't forget to set it right. Otherwise, the rest of the day will be hindered.

Next, wait on God to *worship Him*. Psalms 103, 111, and 145 are wonderful portions to follow as you praise the Lord for the greatness of His power. Or turn to Rev. 4 and 5, and use these passages in your praise to Him. There is no better way to pray scripturally than to pray Scripture.

If you brought a hymnbook you can sing to the Lord. Many wonderful hymns put into words what we could scarcely express ourselves. Maybe you don't sing very well – then be sure you're out of earshot of others as you make a joyful noise to the Lord. *He* will appreciate it.

This will lead you naturally into thanksgiving. Reflect upon the wonderful things God has done for you and thank Him for these – for your own salvation and spiritual blessings, for your family, friends, and opportunities. Go beyond that which you thank the Lord for each day.

As you wait on God, ask for the power of concentration. Bring yourself back from daydreaming.

Pray for Others
Now is the time for unhurried, more detailed prayer for others that you don't get to ordinarily. Remember people in addition to those for whom you usually pray. Trace your way around the world, praying for people by countries. Here are three suggestions as to what to pray:

First, make specific requests for them. Perhaps you remember or have jotted down various needs people have mentioned. Use requests from missionary prayer letters. Pray for their spiritual strength, courage, physical stamina, mental alertness, and so on. Imagine yourself in the situations where these people are, and pray accordingly.

Second, look up some of the prayers in Scripture. Pray what Paul prayed for others in the first chapters of Philippians and Colossians, and in the first and third chapters of Ephesians. This will help you advance in your prayer from the stage of "Lord, bless so and so."

Third, ask for others what you are praying for yourself. Desire for them what the Lord has shown *you*. If you pray a certain verse or promise of Scripture for a person you may want to put the reference by his or her name on your prayer list, and use this verse as you pray for that person the next time. Then use it for thanksgiving as you see the Lord answer.

Pray for Yourself

The third part of your day will be prayer for yourself. If you are facing an important decision you may want to put this before prayer for others.

Again, let your prayer be ordered by Scripture and ask the Lord for understanding according to Ps. 119:18: "Open my eyes that I may see wonderful things in your law." Meditate on Scripture verses you have memorized or promises you have previously claimed from God's Word. Reading through an entire book of the Bible, perhaps aloud, is a good idea. Consider how it applies to your life.

In prayer for yourself, 1 Chron. 4:10 is one good example to follow: Jabez prayed, "Oh that you would bless me and enlarge my territory! Let your hand be with me, and keep me from harm so that I will be free from pain." That's prayer for your personal life, for your growth, for God's presence, and for God's protection. Jabez prayed in the will of God, "and God granted his request."

Your attitude during this portion of your day in prayer should be, "Lord, what do *You* think of my life?" Consider your main objectives in the light of what you know to be God's will for you. Jesus said, "My food is to do the will of him who sent me and to finish his work" (Jn. 4:34). Do you want to do God's will more than anything else?

Then consider your activities—what you *do*—in the context of your objectives. God may speak to you about rearranging your schedule, cutting out certain activities that are good but not the best or some things that are entanglements or impediments to progress. Strip them off. You may be convicted about how you spend your evenings or Saturdays, when you could use the time to advantage and still get the recreation you need.

As you pray, record your thoughts about your activities and use of time, and plan for better scheduling. Perhaps the need for better preparation for your Sunday school class or a personal visit with an individual will come to your mind. Or the Lord may impress you to do something special for someone. Make a note of it.

During this part of your day, bring up any problems or decisions you are facing and seek the mind of God on them. It helps to list the various factors involved. Pray over these and look into the Scriptures for guidance. You may be led to a promise from the passages with which you have already filled your mind during the day.

After prayer, you may reach some definite conclusions on which you can base firm convictions. Your aim in a day of prayer should be to come away with stakes driven—new conclusions, renewed convictions, and specific direction. But don't be discouraged if this is not the case. It may not be God's time for a conclusive answer to your problem. And you may discover that your real need was not to know the next step but to have a new revelation of God himself.

You may want to mark or underline in your Bible the promises God gives you during these protracted times alone, and put the date and a word or two in the margin beside them.

Variety is important. Read a while, pray a while, then walk around. Don't get cramped in one position. As miscellaneous things pop into your mind, either incorporate these into prayer or write them down if they're reminders of something you should do later. Don't just push them aside or they will plague you the rest of the day.

At the end of the day, summarize on paper the things God has spoken to you about. This will be profitable to refer to later. Don't think you must end the day with some extraordinary experience or discovery. The test of the day is not how exhilarated you are when the day is over, but how it works into your life tomorrow.[5]

Chapter 5

WHERE TO GO FOR YOUR PRAYER RETREAT

W e can pray anywhere. That's one of the many wonderful things about our relationship with God. And yet even Jesus, when He wanted deep connection with the Father, "often *withdrew to lonely places and prayed*" (Lk. 5:16, emphasis added). Despite our best intentions (trust me, I have abundant personal experience with this one!), when we try to "retreat" at home or the office, it almost never works. The tyranny of phones, computers, well-meaning visitors, and unfinished projects keeps us from our goal of spending undistracted time in fellowship with the Lord. So where do we go?

I have developed several delightful alternatives over my years of enjoying extended times of prayer with the Lord. A number of Christian camps and conference centers within an hour of where I live offer inexpensive rooms for private retreats. I have several friends who often make their homes available to me while they are away. I've also been to Catholic retreat centers, which can offer an added bonus of interesting prayer opportunities outside my usual tradition (Stations of the Cross, evening vespers, labyrinths, etc.)

Another option I've tried is trading houses with a friend who also enjoys prayer retreats. I don't answer her phone, and she doesn't answer mine. It works well for us! Sometimes I've gone to a church to spend the day. Other times, when the weather has been agreeable, I've gone to a park. I've also rented a hotel room. It hardly matters where you go, so long as it's a quiet, comfortable place where you won't be interrupted or distracted.

Here are some ideas that may help you think through your own options. While I've offered some free and low-cost possibilities, please don't dismiss the idea of budgeting money for a retreat. Remember, time with God is not a luxury, it's a necessity.

FREE

- A friend's vacation home, cabin, condo, or cottage while he or she is away for a weekend
- A chapel or church during the week (check ahead to make sure it will be available and quiet)

INEXPENSIVE

- Catholic retreat centers. Most dioceses have several of these in their district that are usually available to anyone. Call a local Catholic church, or visit www.catholiclinks.org/ retirosunitedstates.htm.
- Christian camps/retreat centers. When they are not having scheduled group activities, many Christian camps are happy to accommodate a personal prayer retreat. Make sure they know this is a personal retreat and you are seeking solitude and quiet. Visit www.ccca.org (Christian Camp and Conference Association) or www.retreatsonline.com/guide/christian.htm for leads. Or check with your own denomination.

PASTORS ONLY

Several ministries offer retreats for pastors, their spouses, and sometimes for other full-time Christian workers very inexpensively or free. Go to www.pastorsretreatnetwork.org or www.nazarenepastor.org. You may also try googling "pastors retreats" for options in various locales and within various denominations. Also, if you'd like a pastors' prayer summit experience (think of it as a guided prayer retreat for pastors and their spouses), check out www.prayersummits.net.

OTHER IDEAS

- Spend the day at a local, state, or national park
- Go camping
- Rent a cabin or cottage
- Go to a resort or spa
- If you have to go away on business, schedule a day or two extra at the beginning or end of your trip

Chapter 6

SHOULD YOU FAST?

I'm often surprised by the number of people who, when I say I'm going on a prayer retreat, take for granted that I will be fasting. For some people the unspoken assumption that they must fast discourages them from getting away with God at all. But it shouldn't! While prayer retreats and fasting *can* go together, they certainly don't have to. Sometimes God will invite you to fast while other times He may invite you to refresh with Him over food.

Every prayer retreat will be different. As with all other aspects of the retreat, it's best to ask God what He wants to do with you on your prayer getaway and let the Holy Spirit guide you. For me, I assume I'll be eating, unless the Holy Spirit specifically directs me to fast.

REASONS TO FAST

With these ideas in mind, a few guidelines about fasting have helped me as I've considered what God wanted to do with me during my prayer retreats. God's Word gives us several principles for when fasting may be appropriate.

Hunger for God
Fasting has a way of helping us really to understand what it means for

our souls and flesh to yearn for God like dry and thirsty lands where there is no water (Ps. 63:1). Every time we feel a pang of hunger, we can direct it into a craving for deeper intimacy with the Lord. Fasting allows us to experience Jesus as our Bread of Life. It helps us to see what Jesus meant when He said, "Man does not live on bread alone but on every word that comes from the mouth of the LORD" (Mt. 4:4).

So if you are feeling a deep desire to know God better and enjoy more intimate fellowship with Him, fasting may be a good tool to help keep that hunger in focus.

Repentance and humility

The only regular fast God required of His people under the Old Covenant was on the Day of Atonement. That day—essentially a prayer retreat on a grand corporate scale—was a day of fasting, repentance, and deep humility. We, too, can benefit when we humble our souls with fasting (see Ps. 35:13, KJV). In Joel 2:12, the prophet suggests that turning to the Lord with repentance, weeping, and mourning may attract the God's pity and favor. "Who knows? He may turn and have pity and leave behind a blessing" (v. 14).

If sin has accumulated in your life, or if you are feeling distanced from God because of failures of any kind, a fast may be a good discipline to add power to your repentance.

Power over temptation

Jesus fortified Himself against temptation with a 40-day fast in the wilderness. Most of us won't be called to fast for that long (and if we are, we should consult a doctor first); however, fasting is a great way to subject our bodies to our spirits. When we fail to discipline our bodies, sin often results. Eve gave up Eden for a taste of forbidden fruit. Esau forfeited his birthright for a bowl of lentil soup. Isaac, hungry for fresh game, blessed the "wrong" son. The Israelites grumbled against God because they wanted meat.

Giving in to our body's every craving makes us sluggish and apathetic.

God warned against this attitude just before bringing the Israelites into the Promised Land. "When you have eaten and are satisfied . . . be careful that you do not forget the LORD your God" (Dt. 8:10-11).

People who struggle with sins of the flesh often will benefit from a time of extended prayer combined with fasting. Denying the flesh in the area of food can help to build discipline that can be applied to other areas of temptation.

In crisis

In Scripture, many times of crisis occurred when people were called to extended times of prayer combined with fasting. Some of these people include the entire nation of Israel under Jehoshaphat's rule, Nehemiah, Esther, Daniel, and the nation of Nineveh (2 Chron. 20:1-4; Neh. 1:4; Est. 4:15-16; Dan. 9:3; Jon. 3:6-9). When we find ourselves in crisis, whether personal or professional or even on a national level, it's probably a good time to add fasting to our prayer retreat.

When we need wisdom

When Daniel sought to understand a perplexing vision, he fasted (Dan. 10). Similarly, when the church in Antioch needed to know whom to send out as missionaries and later whom to appoint as elders in the missionary churches, they met for prayer, worshiping, and fasting (Acts. 13:1-2, 14:23). God loves to give wisdom to those who ask Him for it. Somehow, fasting helps to underscore our sincere reliance on Him.

REASONS NOT TO FAST

There are many reasons not to fast, among these the very practical considerations of one's own health and physical needs. Don't feel guilty if you cannot abstain from food during your prayer retreat. If your getaway is to include food, it's still a good idea to try to keep the fare simple so you can spend your time in prayer rather than in the kitchen. Often my retreat location will offer a refrigerator and microwave, so I bring along bread, cheese, prepared soup, fresh fruits and vegetables, juice, and tea so I won't have to waste prayer time driving around looking for a restaurant or grocery store.

Keep in mind that sometimes God specifically encourages us to eat during our prayer retreats. When may He specifically invite you to eat during your retreat? Here are some specific situations I've discovered.

In times of exhaustion

When Elijah burned out from ministry, he retreated to the desert to be alone with God. There, God miraculously provided him with warm bread and fresh water (1 K. 19:4-9). When we are close to burning out, the Lord delights in restoring us. He does this spiritually and also physically. David describes this well in Psalm 23 where he shows the shepherd leading His sheep into green pastures (read: *sheep food*) and beside still waters so He can restore our souls (vv. 1-3). The last few years have been tough for me as I combined caring for my husband with work. I've had many more prayer retreats that have included eating than ones that have included fasting recently, because the Lord keeps reminding me of His desire to restore me.

When Jesus invites you to deeper intimacy

In Rev. 3:20 we find Jesus longing for us invite Him into our deepest confidence to eat with us and have us eat with Him. Consider taking bread and grape juice or wine along on your prayer retreat to make the experience of this fellowship more meaningful. Enjoy communion—as well as your other meals during the retreat—with Him, as though He were sitting at your table, enjoying a meal and deep conversation with you.

Earlier in this chapter I mentioned that fasting might be a way to symbolize our hunger for deeper intimacy with God. So which is it, fasting or feasting? It depends. Once again, we really need to let the Lord guide us. Ask Him with an open heart, then follow the way He leads. Don't stress about it. We can hardly get it "wrong" when our desire is to fellowship with Him!

In times of thanksgiving and celebration

Like the fast days on the Hebrew calendar, the feast days were times set apart for corporate prayer, worship, thanksgiving, and celebration of God's faithfulness. The Feast of Tabernacles and Pentecost (celebrating the harvest) and Passover and Purim (celebrating God's deliverance) are the most familiar of these. Similarly, we may have times when we will want to retreat with the Lord to reflect on and celebrate His goodness. These times won't be characterized by deprivation.

Undoubtedly, there are many more reasons to fast—or not to—during prayer retreats than mentioned here. The important thing is to let the Holy Spirit direct you. The purpose of your prayer retreat is to have concentrated quality time with the Lord; the food question is secondary to that. So let Him guide you, then relax and just enjoy Him.

Chapter 7

MAKING PRAYER RETREATS A LIFESTYLE

I 'm writing this chapter as I finish up daylong prayer retreat. Honestly, I didn't have time to take this prayer retreat. My desk is piled high at work. I have deadlines looming later this week. And there's no end to the things that need doing at home. But life ganged up on me. It's been more than a month since my last retreat, and in the meantime, I've had a number of disappointments, spiritual attacks, losses, and difficult decisions to make. I tried to handle all of these in my normal prayer times but just couldn't. It was too much. The pressures mounted, my faith made pathetic whimpering sounds, and my prayers grew panicked. I knew I needed extended time with God, and soon.

All this came to a climax yesterday. So I checked my calendar. The only day remotely feasible was today — a mere 18 hours from when I first realized I needed a retreat. Could I make a retreat happen with so little advance warning?

I knew I couldn't arrange for overnight nursing care for my bedridden husband on such quick notice, but I realized that I *could* manage to take the day off from work. Eight hours is less than my preferred overnight retreats but much better than nothing. So I postponed a couple of appointments and notified the folks who needed to know I wouldn't be in to work today.

I then called the church to make an appointment to pray with a pastor first thing in the morning. I don't always do that, but because some of the issues I needed to pray about were warfare, I decided to get some prayer back up. That settled, I then called friends who frequently let me use their home as a retreat spot to make sure it was available. It was. Then I went home and squared away things with my husband's caregivers. This morning I packed my Bible, journal, and worship CDs. I stopped by the church for my prayer appointment, and then dropped by the grocery store to pick up bread and grape juice since I sensed the Lord inviting me to commune with Him.

And here I am. It's been a wonderful day. God has restored my peace, given me fresh perspective and hope, a few assignments, and has otherwise just let me enjoy His presence, encouragement, and strengthening.

If prayer retreats were not my lifestyle, I never would have been able to pull off such a feat. I never would have known it were possible—or even necessary. I wouldn't have known how to prepare. But prayer retreats are part of my spiritual nourishment, discipline, and survival. I can usually tell when I need one, like yesterday. There are certain telltale signs (see below). But even if I don't know I need a prayer retreat, others who know me well do. My friends and family have permission to ask me, "Hey, don't you think you need a prayer retreat soon?" I take them seriously and start making arrangements.

You know it's time for a prayer retreat when . . .

- you're dry and out of touch with the Lord
- you feel overwhelmed, overworked, stressed, or scattered
- you feel mechanical in your devotion and service
- you have an important decision to make
- you have a sinful habit to overcome
- you have a person or people you need to forgive
- you need God's perspective on a situation
- you have a strategic ministry event or season ahead
- you need insight about an unanswered prayer

- you're behind in intercession and others are depending on you
- you haven't had one in three months or more
- your spouse, teenager, roommate, colleague, or dog tells you that you need one

In an ideal world, I would take an overnight retreat once a month and a three-day retreat every quarter. I do not live in that ideal world right now. But it's still a goal of mine, and one day I hope to achieve it. In the meantime, I have made an agreement between myself and God that when He tells me it's time for a getaway with Him, I do it.

I don't know if Jesus followed a disciplined schedule for His prayer retreats, but extended times of prayer and solitude with the Father were His lifestyle. If He, the Son of God, needed them, how much more do we?

I wish we, as Christians, would help each other with this more, as my friend did for me years ago, practically pushing me out of my house to meet with God. Churches and ministries would make a true investment in their staff—and by extension in the kingdom of God—if they provided for them to take regular prayer retreats or even make them part of their job descriptions. Husbands and wives could make their spouses' spiritual health a priority by encouraging and making provision for one another to get regular alone times with God. Friends can trade houses. Small groups can hold each other accountable for individual prayer retreat times. Church prayer ministries can organize corporate prayer retreats where people are taught how to spend extended time with God so that eventually they can feel confident enough to do it on their own.

Prayer retreats provide the time to go deep with God like no other time does. Once you've had your first one or two, you will understand what I mean. They are not a luxury—they are a necessity. They are worth planning and sacrificing for as much as any vacation is and more so, actually. Will you consider making an agreement with the Lord that you will take that important time alone with Him whenever He makes it clear you need to? Or better yet, just schedule it into your life at regular intervals.

Read the following experience of another person who has made prayer retreats a lifestyle.

EXTENDED PRAYER AS A LIFESTYLE
by J. Robb Kelley

I didn't realize I'd been slacking off spiritually. All I knew was that I was exhausted from coaching my high school boys' basketball team through a challenging season. When the buzzer sounded at our last game on a Tuesday night, I felt more like burnt toast than fresh bread. Over the years, I've come to recognize that feeling as the signal that it is time for me to get away alone with God for an extended period of prayer. So I scheduled three days of fasting and praying for the following weekend.

When Friday came, I wasn't sure what to expect. At different times, God meets me in different ways. But this time, almost immediately, God let me know that He meant business. As I prayed, He pointed to area after area in my life. I sensed Him saying that my daily devotions had become lazy and that I was trying to live on spoiled daily manna. He showed me how my tithing had been inconsistent, and He challenged me to become a better steward of my finances. He reminded me that He wanted me to approach those who crossed my path each day with a heart ready to serve. He let me know that if I wanted to receive all He had for me, I would need to be intentional about obeying the truths He'd already taught me in previous years.

If this had been my first prayer retreat, I might not have been able to hear all of this at once. But I've grown gradually over the past 20 years to welcome the conviction of sin — because God always honors repentance by restoring joy, peace, and blessings. In this case, I had a very real sense that God wanted me to become more conscientious in my walk with Him because He was about to unfold something new and special in my life.

When I returned from that prayer retreat, I knew I needed to press in and follow where God was leading. Because I have a flexible work schedule, I was able to set aside extended times of prayer over the next five weeks. During that time, I found myself reading Prov. 31:10-31 about a godly wife. I didn't plan it—that's just where the Spirit kept leading me. *Is that why God wants me to get my life in order?* I wondered. *Does He want to give me a wife?* To make a long story short, three weeks later I met my wife. We were married just under six months after that.

A Healthy Habit

Not all of my prayer retreats have had such dramatic results. But over the 20 years I've been making extended prayer times a lifestyle, God has always done something to bring me closer and more in tune with Him.

My very first prayer retreat grew out of a personal crisis. I had just graduated from college and despite the fact that I'd graduated with honors, I couldn't find a job. I sought God in my usual 5- to 15-minute prayer times, but He was silent. After five months, I was still unemployed—and God was still silent. So with a meager bank account, a surplus of time on my hands, and a whole lot at stake, I tried setting aside entire days and nights to seek God.

I read my Bible for hours. I took long prayerwalks, day and night. I shot hoops in my backyard and cried out to God. I took two- to three-hour bike rides, asking Him to speak to my heart. After many months of extended times of prayer, I finally began to sense God speaking to me. Eventually, He led me unmistakably to my first job, where He surprised and favored me with a promotion after I'd worked only three months.

In the years since, my prayer retreats have taken many forms. I don't usually go with an agenda. Instead, I let the Lord give me a Bible verse to meditate on, bring to mind a situation He wants me to act upon, or show me how to prepare for an upcoming event. Sometimes,

He addresses sins I need to repent of. Other times, He leads me to pray for someone in need or to contact and encourage someone. The extended time also gives me plenty of opportunity to interact with God in His Word and to worship Him.

Sometimes I spend my prayer retreats alone at home. Other times I go on long drives, take a weekend road trip, or sit in an empty church. On some occasions, I get a hotel room for the weekend, go camping in the wilderness, or go to my church's retreat center. Other times, I might join a small group of men who are gathering to meet with God.

My barometer for extended prayer is usually either the need to make an important decision or an obvious lack of the fruit of the Spirit in my life (Gal. 5:22-23). For example, I noticed recently that I responded poorly to my wife about a financial decision we were discussing. At work, I was short with a fellow employee. Then I observed I had a general lack of peace and joy in my life. That very week I took a day to be alone with God. After that, my whole emotional state was renewed and my relationships were restored to include more love, understanding, and patience.

I usually take extended prayer times to prepare for speaking engagements and ministry tasks as well. God uses those times to get me ready for however He is going to use me to meet the needs of His people.

Making the Time

Finding room in packed schedules for extended prayer sessions can be challenging. In the beginning, what helped me the most was examining where I spent my time and evaluating what that said about my priorities. I wrote up a prayer retreat schedule to help me be more disciplined. Then I shared with my family, friends, and coworkers why I was setting aside extended time to seek God's heart. I kept coming across a certain verse that came into my heart with the intensity of a command and strengthened my resolve: "But seek first his kingdom and his righteousness, and all these things will be given to you as well" (Mt. 6:33).

Through a lifestyle of extended prayer retreats, God has shown me a pathway into the unfathomable riches of intimacy with Him. The abundance that Jesus talks about, the fullness that He purchased for us on the cross, the life I had longed for finally opened up for me when I discovered the hidden treasures of personal prayer retreats.[6]

Chapter 8

TAKING OTHERS ALONG

T ime alone with God has been the secret to my spiritual health. In the fiercest storms, God has kept me steady, rooted in Him. When the winds start to blow, I get out my calendar and schedule time with Him and He gives me whatever I need — guidance, reassurance, renewed faith, comfort, insight, spiritual rest, and much more.

Because I know how much God has given to me when I have given extended time to Him, I want to share this secret with others. Whenever I see friends struggling, overwhelmed, or discouraged, I'm likely to ask, "Have you gotten away alone with God recently?" Prayer retreats are too valuable a thing to keep a secret.

Over the years I've helped others to take prayer retreats, too. Sometimes I take a small group, such as the *Pray!* magazine staff, to a quiet place where I can guide them in private and shared prayer times with God. Other times I seek God on behalf of a friend and then give that person a personalized guide with Scripture suggestions, prayer activities, and questions to enhance his or her hearing from God about a particular issue.

I have friends who take larger groups on prayer retreats. Pastor Buddy Westbrook makes prayer retreats a regular part of his church leadership's spiritual life. Steve Brooks took prayer retreats to the denominational level of his church. J. Robb Kelley and Gary Skinner do retreats with small groups of men. Gary's wife, Susan, did it with a small group of widows.

What follows are some of their stories, along with resources and ideas.

Now that you are enjoying extended times with God, why not give the gift of prayer retreats to friends and people you care about?

Introducing Men to Prayer Retreats
by J. Robb Kelley

A few years ago I met a man who was literally at his wit's end. He had experienced some tragic losses and devastating failures over the years, and he was driving across the country looking for a reason to continue living. He ended up in our church parking lot on a Wednesday after spotting the cross on top of our worship center. By Friday, he was driving out to a prayer retreat with me and eight other men he'd never met. After three days of prayer, worship, Bible study, and fellowship, he had a life-changing encounter with God that turned everything around for him.

Under ordinary circumstances, I'm pretty sure this man wouldn't have come to a prayer retreat. When life is going well, most men are not naturally drawn to silence and solitude. Maybe we'll go to a morning prayer meeting with other guys. But taking time out for lengthy sessions of prayer and Bible reading until we receive breakthroughs? Most of us aren't inclined that way.

Two Motivations
A while back, a friend, who is a pastor, and I felt that we needed to introduce more men to prayer retreats. We wanted them to have the time to cultivate a deeper relationship with God and get that experience of hearing God speak into the big issues of their lives. But how could we get them interested?

Over time, we learned that two things really motivate men to try an extended time of prayer. The first is the example of other men. The second is crisis.

Our home church has a culture of prayer. Our senior pastor regularly encourages us to get away, even to reserve a cabin in the wilderness for a focused time of prayer. In fact, for most of our pastors, prayer retreats are an annual, quarterly, or even monthly activity. Seeing this example has inspired many men I know to try an extended time of prayer. They know that others have met God during prayer retreats; maybe they will meet Him, too.

As far as crises go, most of us don't plan for those—they just come. Our experience has been, more often than not, that if you find a Christian man in crisis and offer him a prayer retreat—especially if the invitation is backed up by your own testimony of what God has done for you during times of extended prayer—he'll come.

But just getting men to come to a prayer retreat isn't enough. As my friend and I began leading these retreats, we learned that it was necessary to coach the men on what is involved in a personal prayer retreat.

We led them in times of corporate praise and worship. We encouraged them to go off and read their Bibles alone; then we'd all come back together and share what we thought God was speaking to us. We suggested individual prayerwalks, where we focused on listening for impressions or directions God might bring to our hearts. We led group discussion times where we could share openly and honestly about anything and receive prayer from each other.

Becoming Transparent

During these retreats, it didn't take long for the men to drop their guards—because we all so clearly saw God moving in our midst. At times, His presence was obvious in the calm that permeated the room. Other times, the prayers over one of the men would hit the mark exactly and bring healing, comfort, wisdom, understanding, or direction. Often, a deep, supernatural peace would fill our hearts.

At several of these prayer retreats, God has honored Jas. 5:16 in a powerful way: "Therefore confess your sins to each other and pray for each other so that you may be healed." Finding the capacity to be transparent before God and others can be extremely difficult for men. Yet it is the gateway to unfathomable riches. We've seen divorces avoided and marriages restored through personal prayer retreats. We've seen physical healings take place. We've had fathers reconcile with their children and their own parents. At these retreats many have decided to set out on a better or new career path or found the peace and direction needed to make a major life decision. Others have had a life-changing encounter with God that propelled them to greater intimacy with Him.

We've heard men say over and over again that their first prayer retreat was a significant milestone on their journey of faith. For many of them, the retreat was the first time they had ever spent a whole weekend seeking God. But for most of them, it was not to be their last.[7]

TAKING IT ON THE ROAD
by Gary Skinner

Over the past few years, I have been doing weekend retreats in the mountains with groups of 8 to 12 men. I like to take at least two men with me who are close friends and know what to expect. The rest can be men I know little or nothing about. In reality, these are prayer retreats, but we never call them that. We want to attract guys who truly need this kind of getaway but would not normally be interested in a prayer retreat.

What We Do
We usually arrive on a Thursday evening, share dinner, learn a little about each other, pray together a little, and then get some sleep. On Friday morning, I go over some Scriptures and then teach on how to listen for God through the Scriptures. I always hone in on the value of getting on the floor to wait on God.

I know that the floor thing is too big a jump for some men. So I tell them they can go for a walk or sit under a tree if they prefer – just as long as they are comfortable and quiet and able to let their hearts be open to the Holy Spirit. I usually tell them my story, emphasize the importance of honesty and humility before God, and then encourage them to go out and try it.

On Friday evening, we have an opportunity to share with the group what happened or didn't happen. What we hear, almost always, is absolutely amazing. In general, three themes usually surface in the testimonies – and often confessions – from the men: an acknowledgement of an area in their lives that God wants to improve, a true sense of forgiveness from God for where they have fallen short, and a fresh vision and hope for the future. What is most fascinating to me is that this all takes place without a sermon or lecture. They get it directly from God.[8]

LEADING WOMEN IN PRAYER RETREATS
by Susan Skinner

Six years ago, I found myself in the interesting situation of leading a group for widows. I am not a widow. About all I had in common with these women was that I was a woman!

Nevertheless, the eight ladies who joined were thrilled to have a group created just for them. They ranged in age from 30 to 70 years old. I quickly became their emotional support and daily sounding board. The problem was that I did not have the resources or the experience to meet their considerable needs. I didn't have a clue about how to help them, and I was on my way to being completely overwhelmed.

Around that time, I took one of my monthly retreats for three days of prayer and fasting. I definitely needed to be refreshed! It was during this time that the Lord gave me a solution for the widows. He said, *Susan, you can't fix these women. But I can. You need to bring them to Me. Why don't you invite them up here each month when you come? Teach them how to seek Me, how to know Me personally, and how to hear what I have to say to them. Then they can build a trust in Me only. Their whole prayer life will change, and the pressure won't be on you.* A light went on inside me as I listened to Him, and I felt a huge weight being lifted off of me.

Connecting with God

The next month, I invited the women to come with me to pray and fast. Not all of them came. But those who did began the transformation process almost immediately. I encouraged them to spend time alone with the Lord. They could rest, read, walk, or just sit before the Lord. I asked them to write down anything they sensed from God during that time. Then we would get together in the evenings to share.

Tears and joy flowed as we saw how God was working in each woman. One woman said she had not heard from the Lord since her husband died years before. Another woman said God told her she would find joy in working as a hairdresser to support her young children. Another said she felt His comfort, and He had set her free from a deep grief that had lasted for 35 years. All the women said they saw God in a new light. They saw how much He loved them and that He still had a plan for their lives.

After about four months, the group dissolved. The need was no longer there, because they had found Jesus in a personal way and were walking hand in hand with Him. Our friendships continue, but they are not based on the original intention of the group. And I can say with confidence that all of the women who went on that prayer retreat are staying connected with God. Some have remarried, others have not; but all are enjoying the fruit of transformation that comes from spending time away with the Lord.

Now when I encounter people with big needs, I confidently tell them that I have no clue how to help them, but I know Someone who does. God once told me that I'm like the tow truck and He's the mechanic. I just tow the broken people to Him. He's the one who does the fixing.[9]

DISCERNING GOD'S LEADING FOR YOUR CHURCH
by Buddy Westbrook

As I pastor, I've been involved in countless meetings where we prayed before we got started, handled our business, and then asked God to bless whatever we decided. But when a group of us started a church several years ago, we committed ourselves to a different plan for church leadership. Instead of deciding what we thought was right and then asking God to bless it, we determined that we would ask God what He wanted to do — and then we would do that.

We called ourselves "decision-discerners," because we felt that our job was to discern His decisions rather than make decisions. We quickly learned, however, that a two-hour meeting was not enough time to hear adequately from God. So, from our church's infancy, my elder team and I have made a commitment to prayer retreats.

We regularly bring our ministries and leaders before the Lord in prayer and attempt to listen for His perspective and directions.

A Difficult Decision

Last February we did this with our worship ministry. As is our custom, we sought Him individually during the week, asking for His input on this ministry. This time, we all sensed the Lord saying that He had much to say and wanted to meet with us all together. We were a little surprised because, frankly, the worship ministry seemed to be going well. However, we all took a day off from work for extended prayer and fasting.

When we met together that Thursday morning, we had a time of confession to remove any prayer hindrances. We followed that with worship. After worship, we took turns sharing what we had heard

from the Lord on our own — something we've come to call the "whats."
For example, when God called Abram (Gen. 12:1-5), He only revealed
the "what" — "I will make you into a great nation." The "how" was left
for later. Nevertheless, Abram believed the Lord and ventured out.
The Lord has taught us to listen carefully to the "whats" before we
pursue any "hows."

In this case, we discerned that the "what" had to do with our
worship minister, but we did not know what this meant. So we broke
for individual time with God, asking Him to clarify the "whats" and
redirect us. We each took "dialogue" notes, where we wrote what
we asked or said to God and then recorded what we believe He said
in response. We also asked Him to reveal or highlight anything we
especially needed to hear.

When we reconvened, we all believed we had heard the Lord
say the same thing: that He was doing behind-the-scenes work that
would require changes and that He had been withholding His power
from the worship ministry until these changes were made. Two of our
elders recorded identical instructions from the Lord: that we were
to release our worship minister because there were new gifts and
directions that God had chosen for the ministry.

Such a radical and unexpected directive from the Lord unsettled
us. But all the elders had heard pieces that confirmed the overall
message. As we digested the idea over the next couple of days, the
Lord gradually and creatively showed us the "hows" — how we would
need to go about implementing this difficult change. He gave us a
gracious way to share the news with our worship minister, who, after
praying, confirmed that indeed this was the Lord's word for us and
willingly shared that assurance with the congregation.

Since that time, God has been releasing His power over our worship
in impressive ways. Musicians and singers are using their gifts in
ways we (and they!) did not know were possible. As a congregation,
we are connecting with the Lord, enjoying His presence, and sensing
His pleasure in much fuller ways.

Leading the Way

We consistently use prayer retreats to discern God's leading when hiring staff, exploring issues, exercising church discipline, or planning expansion. Our elders know before they come on board that periodic prayer retreats are part of their job description. It seems to be something they look forward to.

I believe that the Lord God desires to release His power in unprecedented ways in today's church. But we need to be able to listen well in order to follow His instructions. That's where prayer retreats are foundational. They are a practical way to open the church to His authority and His lordship — by putting us in the role of decision-discerners instead of decision makers.[10]

DENOMINATION REJUVENATION
by Steve Brooks

Six years ago, I never would have considered myself a prayer leader. I was a pastor and, at the time, the vice president of the Reformed Church of America (RCA) with its 950 churches. But I have to admit that I struggled with prayer.

I would classify myself as a Type A personality. So when I first came into my denominational leadership role, I was full of great ideas about what our churches needed to recapture their call to life and mission. God, however, confirmed none of my ideas! Instead, He gave me a prayer partner — another pastor who regularly telephoned me to pray. As we prayed, God reminded us of a vision that He had given our church in 2000: to become a denomination made up of individual houses of prayer. But we had no idea how He wanted to accomplish such a major shift.

Then, in 2001 when I was the newly elected denominational president, the Holy Spirit whispered a reminder to me during our General Synod meetings: *Brooks, I'm serious about this house of prayer thing.* I was humbled, because God had just begun to teach me to pray — and it had not been easy to get me to slow down enough to do it. How could we get an entire denomination there?

Houses of Prayer

I had been asking God to revive our denomination. And since He didn't seem to be too hot about any of my ideas, I decided I'd better start following some of His. So I called for a prayer retreat.

Twelve of us from all over the nation gathered at a retreat center. Since God was calling our denomination to prayer, we figured that prayer is where we should begin. We had no idea how God would lead; all we knew was that we were supposed to seek Him and His will on how to become a denomination of houses of prayer.

During our three days together, we worshiped, shared our stories, built relationships, and sought the Lord's face. Sometimes we would spend more than two hours in prayer before someone would offer an impression about how we might move forward. During that retreat, God led us to the idea of local church prayer leaders, a new concept for the RCA. We discerned that God was leading us to serve the RCA, but not necessarily using traditional models. We had to work through some tension between those who had strong ties to denominational traditions and those who did not. Somehow, laying these issues before the Lord together established our communication with and trust in one another.

Continuing On

Over the next three years, we continued to meet at prayer retreats, and God continued to give us very specific direction. He led us to identify local church prayer leaders in every church in the denomination. He revealed a plan for equipping those leaders. He encouraged us to pray blessing on the intercessors in our denomination. And He eventually guided us to create a staff position for a denominational prayer leader who would encourage and equip the local church prayer leaders.

We continue to hold prayer retreats once or twice a year. We realize that we cannot fulfill God's purposes with our own ideas—we need to seek Him together for His will and ways. In the five years since that initial prayer retreat, we have identified 250 local church prayer leaders. Prayer is permeating our denomination. Our most recent General Synod meeting had 24/7 prayer coverage from all across North America. God has led us to plant 400 new churches by 2013. Pastors are gathering for prayer, and their churches are getting healthier every day.

Prayer retreats are not just for individuals or church groups. God is reviving an entire denomination that had grown stagnant. And He's using prayer retreats to lead and inspire the denomination's leaders in His renewing work.[11]

SING YOUR PRAYERS
by Brenda Poinsett

A while ago, I noticed that a number of women in my church seemed to be carrying heavy burdens. Knowing that they probably needed time to connect with the Lord in prayer but were very busy, I invited them to a "Sabbath of Song," a prayer retreat where we would sing our prayers to God.

Prior to this Saturday morning event, our choir director, a guitarist, and I met to plan the day. We selected hymns or prayer songs that directly addressed God and grouped them by theme. Then we chose Scripture that related to each theme. For songs of praise and thanksgiving, we chose Scriptures from the psalms. For songs that expressed strong emotion—both positive and negative—we picked corresponding texts that showed people such as Moses, Hannah, and David praying. And for songs that bolstered faith in difficult times, we selected the accounts of Judah's army meeting its enemy with songs and praise (2 Chron. 20:21-30) and Paul and Silas singing in prison (Acts 16:25-34).

We printed the words to the songs and gave them to the women as they arrived at the little rural church we'd secured for the occasion. We began with a light breakfast, then for the first hour, we sang praise and thanksgiving songs. We also read the psalms responsively, mentioning that many of them had been written originally as prayer songs.

We followed this by offering a 25-minute period for the women to go outside for individual prayer focusing on Psalm 30, a prayer song that closes with, "You turned my wailing into dancing; you removed my sackcloth and clothed me with joy, that my heart may sing to you and not be silent" (vv. 11-12). After that, we came back together and spent the last hour singing the remaining songs and telling the stories of the Bible characters who sang similar prayers. We ended at noon with lunch.

As we finished our time together, one woman said that God had used the time to reassure her that He was still working in her life. Another said she experienced a new level of communion with Him. As the women left, their faces showed that the "Sabbath of Song" had indeed refreshed them.[12]

PRAYER SUMMITS ARE FOR EVERYONE
by Dennis Fuqua

Since pastors' prayer summits were introduced, thousands of pastors across the world have been refreshed, realigned, and re-energized in their prayer lives. Taking the next step, many of them are starting to lead congregations in a similar prayer summit experience.

What Is a Prayer Summit?

A congregational prayer summit is a multi-day worship experience that implements the concept of "Spirit-led, worship-fed, corporate prayer." This prayer retreat is Spirit-led, as opposed to pre-planned; it's worship-fed, as opposed to request-driven. It's corporate prayer, as opposed to individual prayers offered in a group setting. The sole purpose is to seek God, His kingdom, and His righteousness with the expectation that He will guide the group through a humbling, healing, uniting process that will lead them to unity of heart, mind, and mission.

Why Host a Prayer Summit?

Prayer summits aren't about working harder at prayer but becoming more delighted – and thus more effective – in it. A prayer summit is an environment for people to learn the delight of corporate, worship-based prayer while providing an opportunity for leaders and the congregation to have a common experience related to prayer. During a summit, the attendees can hear from God's heart and receive His passion for the world. In addition, leaders can live out the commitment of Acts 6:4 by "giving [their] attention to prayer and the ministry of the word."

Hosting a prayer summit allows for an extended time for Jesus to be at the center and the pastor to facilitate the process of all the people focusing on and moving toward Him. It also allows for various gifts to be used and appreciated and different perspectives to be shared and valued. Everyone can participate in and contribute to the flow of the meeting in a meaningful and significant way.

I remember watching a participant of a prayer summit looking at the pastor with tears in her eyes. "Pastor, thank you so much for helping me love Jesus through worship-based prayer," she said. At a men's summit, one man said, "I had no idea how we were going to spend eight hours praying; but this ended up being too short!"[13]

HEARING GOD THROUGH SCRIPTURES

by Gary Skinner

W hen I mentor people at prayer retreats, I'm often asked, "Can each of us hear from God?" I believe we can. Here is a simple exercise I've encouraged hundreds of people to try with great success.

1. Find a quiet place to be alone.
2. Get in a comfortable position that is conducive for reading and writing.
3. Begin with prayer
   - Deal honestly and openly with God regarding any unconfessed sin in your life.
   - Read Eph. 1:17-18, then ask God to enlighten your understanding and make the words come alive in your heart.
   - Ask God to teach you through the Holy Spirit; ask Him what He wants you to learn today.
4. Leave behind your agendas. Your goal is to hear whatever God wants to tell you, not to get an answer to a specific problem.
5. Read Scripture. A good starting place for many people is the Sermon on the Mount (Mt. 5–7).

6. Take your time. Read slowly, often taking a moment or two to close your eyes and let the words sink in. Do not be discouraged if nothing jumps out at you immediately. When you come to something that you believe is speaking to your heart, write down what you think God might be saying to you.

7. Write down everything that comes to your mind. Part of hearing God's voice is learning how to distinguish His voice from other thoughts. As you look over your notes later, you will find some of it amazingly and obviously God—and some of it humorously foolish. Often your first experience of clear communication from God will be something simple like a leading to ask for forgiveness from someone or to send a note of thanks. As you do this exercise more often, you will find that the Scriptures come alive in a personal way, bringing your relationship with Jesus Christ to a greater depth of friendship, worship, and intimacy.

8. Always remember, God wants a relationship with you. He wants you to hear and understand Him. "My sheep listen to my voice; I know them, and they follow me" (Jn. 10:27).[14]

PERSONAL PRAYER
RETREAT QUESTIONS

S ometimes a friend may need a prayer retreat for a very specific purpose. You may want to ask God to give you a plan to help your friend design a special retreat. That happened to me not long ago. A friend of mine was considering marriage. Pastor Buddy Westbrook and I prayerfully sought the Lord on her behalf, asking Him to give us questions that would help her hear from Him. Here's what He gave us to share with her.

A PRAYER RETREAT BEFORE MARRIAGE

This retreat is designed for you to get alone with God. Your partner should have his own time with God separate from yours. After the two of you have met with the Lord individually, schedule a time to share together what you each heard Him say. Ask a minimum of 3-5 people to pray for you during the length of your retreat. Have them pray that you will be able to relax; to speak openly, honestly, and vulnerably to God; and to hear Him speak clearly to you.

You are not necessarily asking Him to give you a "Yes, you should marry," or "No, you should not marry" answer at this point. Rather, you are to have a loving Father-daughter conversation in which you share your heart with Him and He shares His heart with you. Listen well. God will most likely speak to you with affection, complete thoughts, deep emotions, and incredible understanding. If at any point you feel uncomfortable with how the conversation is going, tell Him. And let Him talk to you about the communication process itself.

Begin your time with worship. Actively listen to worship music or even better, sing. Read at least one psalm (consider reading 103, 111, 121, 145, or 147). Share with God what is meaningful to you about this psalm.

Next, read Psalm 139 and spend some time confessing and dealing with any blockages between you and God. Experience His forgiveness.

Prayerfully consider these questions and journal what you hear.

- Do you think God brought you together? Why?
- What would God say His purpose for this relationship is?
- What goals might He want to accomplish in you through it?
- What goals might He want to accomplish in your partner?
- What goals might He want to accomplish in and through the relationship itself?
- What weaknesses or patterns do you possess that could misdirect this relationship?
- How can you uniquely minister to your partner?
- How can your partner uniquely minister to you?
- How can God be the head of this relationship? How can this be evaluated?
- Do you have any sense that God's purposes for this relationship may already or are soon to be completed? If you answered "yes," then what might God say was the purpose for this short-term relationship? What words might He as your loving Father use to communicate this to you?

Feel free to take breaks during your retreat time. You could take a walk, listen to worship music, or take a nap. At the end of your retreat, write a summary of what God is saying and how He seems to be leading you. Thank Him for speaking to You.

LECTIO DIVINA

ectio Divina is Latin for "divine reading," a nearly 1,000-year-old
Christian method of reading and praying Scripture for the purpose
of life transformation. James Wakefield, author of *Sacred Listening:
Discovering the Spiritual Exercises of Ignatius Loyola,* describes the
process:

> There are four parts to our sacred listening with Holy Scripture:
> In the *lectio*, we read the text slowly, out loud if possible, and then
> sit in silence for several minutes. In the *meditatio*, we consider
> the text with our imagination and heart. Try to witness a scene
> by taking a particular point of view or role in your imagination.
> Sit in silence with the scene until you are moved to speak about
> it with the Lord.
>
> In the *oratio*, we discuss the text and our response with the
> Lord. You will learn to follow the Holy Spirit as you ask for Jesus'
> help, correction, and guidance in living consistently with His
> will in your lifelong contemplation of the text. The *contemplatio*
> is the lifelong experience of discovering how the text shapes us
> within our communities and within the kingdom of God.

Here's how you do it: Read the text out loud and wait in silence for three or four minutes. Use your imagination to enter the text as fully as possible. Do not try to analyze or decipher its meanings. Rather, allow it to impact your heart and emotions. Repeat this reading and silent waiting twice. Jot down what you experienced.

Now respond to the Lord in prayer. Tell Him what you are feeling about this passage and the way you experienced it. Express your longings, fears, hopes, frustrations, etc. Be very honest. Record your prayer or a summary of it in your notebook.

The following day (or in a retreat setting, before you begin your next reading), do the *contemplatio* by reflecting on how the Holy Spirit brought the passage and your prayers to mind and actual experience. Record your feelings about your responses in your notebook.

SAMPLE SCHEDULE FOR A GROUP RETREAT

H ere is the group-retreat schedule my staff and I enjoyed one fall. Our focus was rest and refreshment, and our method was *lectio divina*, an ancient method of reading and praying with Scripture. I printed out the texts ahead of time so the group didn't have to flip pages in their Bibles. This schedule can be adapted for your group's needs.

MONDAY

2:30 p.m. Arrive
3:15 p.m. Gather. Talk about our hopes, expectations, and fears about this retreat time. Share experiences from other prayer retreats. Introduce God's purposes for us for this retreat: Protection, Presence, Rest, Refreshment, Peace, and Provision. Pray the Lord's Prayer together, expanding and personalizing each section, and interceding for each other on each point as the Holy Spirit leads.
5:00 p.m. Dinner prep
5:30 p.m. Dinner
6:45 p.m. *GodViews* video/popcorn, followed by discussion and brief prayer time asking God to reveal Himself to us more clearly and

accurately and to correct our false notions about Him.

8 p.m. Free time

TUESDAY

8 a.m. Breakfast

9:15 a.m. Group lectio with Hagar (Gen. 16:1-16; 21:1-21; 25:12-17). Our focus is Protection and Presence and trying to experience God caring for us this way.

10:30 a.m. Lectio with Mt. 11:28-29 and Psalm 23. Our focus is Rest and Refreshment. Personal time with the Lord.

11:30 a.m. Gather to discuss what we heard/received from the Lord.

12 p.m. Lunch

1 p.m. Free time

2:15 p.m. Lectio with Lk. 12:22-34. Our focus is Provision. Personal time with the Lord.

3:15 p.m. Meet to discuss our experiences with the Lord over this passage, to thank Him, and to pray for one another about what He's given to us during the retreat in general.

4 p.m. Free time

4:30 p.m. Depart

NOTES

1. Sanny, Lorne, "How to Spend a Day in Prayer." *Discipleship Journal*, January/February 1982.
2. Skinner, Gary, "A Place of Transformation," *Pray!* January/February 2007.
3. LaFountain, Richard, "Within Reach," *Pray!* January/February 2004.
4. Collins Pratt, Lonni, "A Day to Pray," *Discipleship Journal* January/February 1996.
5. Sanny, Lorne, "How to Spend a Day in Prayer," *Discipleship Journal* January/February 1982.
6. Kelley, J. Robb, "Repeat as Needed," *Pray!* January/February 2007.
7. Kelley, J. Robb, "An Invitation to Encounter God," *Pray!* January/February 2007.
8. Skinner, Gary, "A Place of Transformation," *Pray!* January/February 2007.
9. Skinner, Susan, "Bring Them to Me," *Pray!* January/February 2007.
10. Westbrook, Buddy, "Decisions, Decisions," *Pray!* January/February 2007.
11. Brooks, Steve, "Denomination Rejuvenation." *Pray!* January/February 2007.

12. Poinsett, Brenda, "Sing Your Prayers in a Sabbath of Song," *Pray!* November/December 2006.

13. Fuqua, Dennis, "Prayer Summits Are for Everyone," *Pray!* May/June 2005.

14. Skinner, Gary, "Hearing God through the Scriptures," *Pray!* January/February 2007.

Do you need more resources on prayer? Check out these NavPress titles!

Intercessors Arise
Debbie Przybylski
978-1-60006-223-0
1-60006-223-7

Imagine watching whole neighborhoods affected, cities and nations touched by the power of prayer. With the key concepts taught in Intercessors Arise, you'll learn to release your potential in prayer through practical and personal application steps. Use it alone or with a group, and stand in the gap for a world in need of change.

Lord, Teach Us to Pray
Fred A. Hartley III
978-1-57683-441-1
1-57683-441-7

Sit at the feet of the Master Pray-er, where you'll learn mountain-quaking, heaven-moving, hell-binding, life-transforming prayer. Just five little words will turn your world right-side up — and lead you into an enjoyment of God you never imagined possible.

Prayer on Fire
Fred A. Hartley III
978-1-57683-960-7
1-57683-960-5

Prayer On Fire is what happens when your initiative to meet with God in prayer connects with his initiative to meet you with His passionate presence. Discover how God calls His people to expect, welcome, and invite His presence in their prayers through the Holy Spirit.

To order copies, visit your local Christian bookstore, call NavPress at 1-800-366-7788, or log on to www.navpress.com.

To locate a Christian bookstore near you, call 1-800-991-7747.

Here's a resource to help you pray with more
Power, Passion, & Purpose

Every issue of *Pray!* is filled with outstanding content:

- Powerful teaching by seasoned intercessors and prayer leaders

- Encouragement and insight to help you grow in your prayer life—no matter at what level you are currently

- Exciting news stories on the prayer movement and prayer events around the world

- Profiles on people, organizations, and churches with unique prayer ministries

- Practical ideas to help you become a more effective pray-er

- Inspirational columns to stimulate you to more passionate worship of Christ

- Classic writings by powerful intercessors of the past

- And much, much more!

No Christian who wants to pray more powerfully and effectively should be without *Pray!*

Six issues of *Pray!* ® are only $21.97*

(Canadian and international subscriptions are only $29.97)

*plus sales tax where applicable

Call **1-800-691-PRAY** (or 1-515-242-0297)
and mention code H8PRBK when you place your order.